C000177798

44

£17·99

# LEEDS PUBS AND CINEMAS BY TRAM

## JIM SOPER

A Horsfield tram advertising Melbourne Ales is standing at "Another Melbourne House", the Junction Hotel at the junction of Dewsbury Road and Moor Road.  In 1960 the Melbourne Brewery was purchased by Joshua Tetley & Son of Leeds.                              Date: 9 August 1956.

Published by the Leeds Transport Historical Society 2019

A Society for the study and preservation of local passenger transport
Charitable Incorporated Organisation No. 1160466

Registered Address: 16 Sussex Avenue, Horsforth, LS18 5NP.

Printed by The Amadeus Press,
Cleckheaton. BD19 4TQ

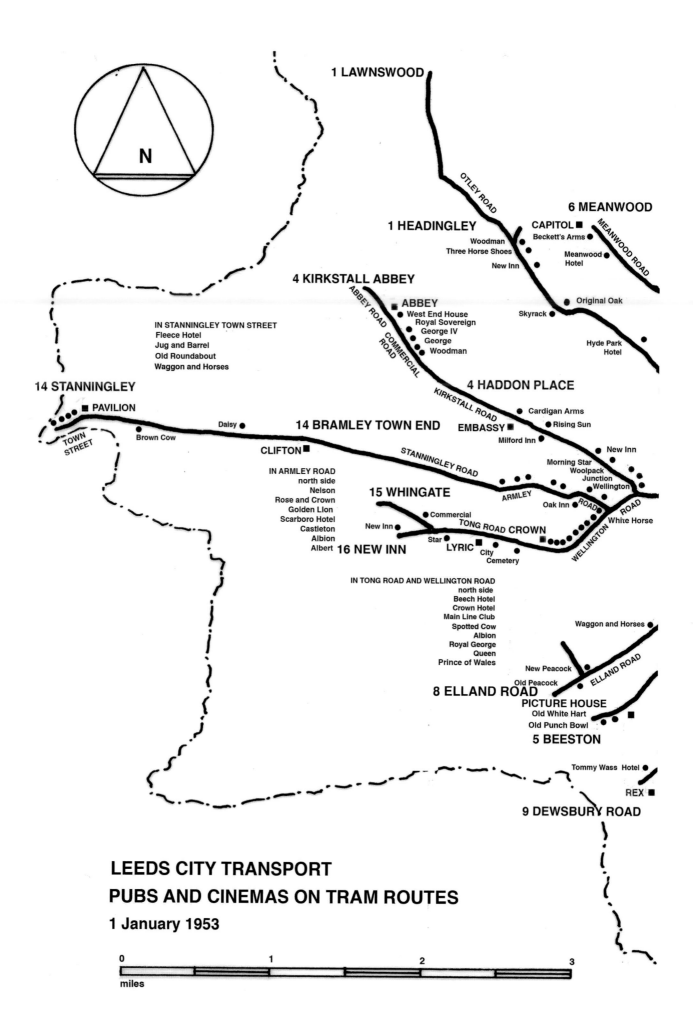

**1 LAWNSWOOD**

**6 MEANWOOD**

OTLEY ROAD

**1 HEADINGLEY**

CAPITOL ■

MEANWOOD ROAD

Beckett's Arms ●

Woodman ●

Three Horse Shoes ●

Meanwood ● Hotel

New Inn ●

**4 KIRKSTALL ABBEY**

ABBEY ROAD

ABBEY ■

West End House ●

Royal Sovereign ●

Original Oak ●

George IV ●

Skyrack ●

COMMERCIAL ROAD

George ●

Woodman ●

Hyde Park Hotel ●

IN STANNINGLEY TOWN STREET
Fleece Hotel
Jug and Barrel
Old Roundabout
Waggon and Horses

KIRKSTALL ROAD

**4 HADDON PLACE**

**14 STANNINGLEY**

Cardigan Arms ●

PAVILION ■

Daisy ●

**14 BRAMLEY TOWN END**

EMBASSY ■

Rising Sun ●

Milford Inn ●

New Inn ●

TOWN STREET

Brown Cow ●

CLIFTON ■

STANNINGLEY ROAD

Morning Star ●

Woolpack ●

Junction ●

IN ARMLEY ROAD
north side
Nelson
Rose and Crown
Golden Lion
Scarboro Hotel
Castleton
Albion
Albert

**15 WHINGATE**

Wellington ●

ARMLEY

Oak Inn ●

ROAD

ROAD

New Inn ●

Commercial ●

TONG ROAD   CROWN ■

White Horse ●

Star ●

LYRIC ■

**16 NEW INN**

City Cemetery

WELLINGTON ROAD

IN TONG ROAD AND WELLINGTON ROAD
north side
Beech Hotel
Crown Hotel
Main Line Club
Spotted Cow
Albion
Royal George
Queen
Prince of Wales

Waggon and Horses ●

New Peacock ●

ELLAND ROAD

Old Peacock ●

**8 ELLAND ROAD**

PICTURE HOUSE

Old White Hart ●

■

Old Punch Bowl ●

**5 BEESTON**

Tommy Wass Hotel ●

REX ■

**9 DEWSBURY ROAD**

# LEEDS CITY TRANSPORT
# PUBS AND CINEMAS ON TRAM ROUTES
### 1 January 1953

0        1        2        3

miles

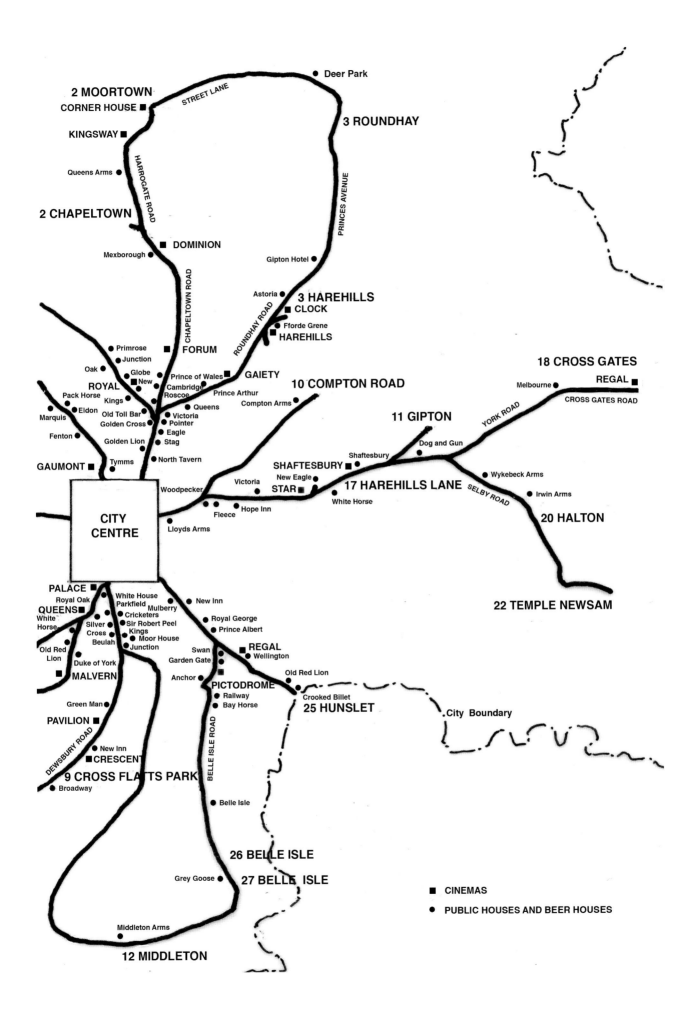

iii

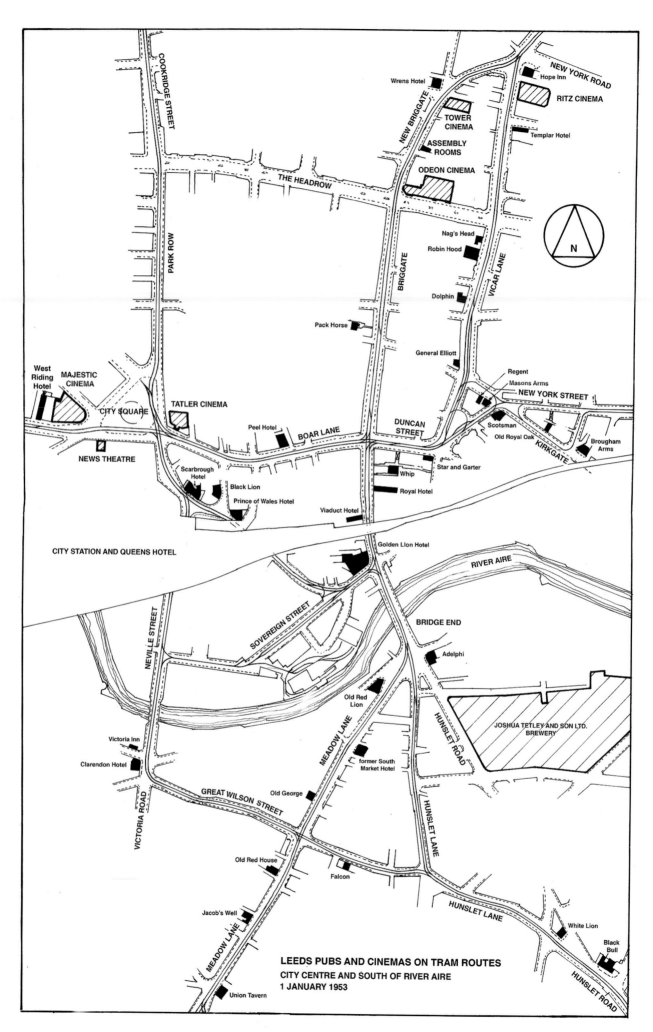

LEEDS PUBS AND CINEMAS ON TRAM ROUTES
CITY CENTRE AND SOUTH OF RIVER AIRE
1 JANUARY 1953

# INTRODUCTION

For this publication the Leeds Transport Historical Society has to thank the Leeds tramway and bus photographers of the 1950's: Bob Mack, David Packer, Bob Parr, Colin Routh, Jim Soper, Keith Terry, Chris Thornburn and one or two others. From 1953 the tramways were progressively abandoned and attempts were made to photograph the Leeds trams and tram routes from every possible angle and sometimes intentionally, but more often than not unintentionally, included many of the long gone old pubs and cinemas that were to be seen on the various tram routes. Between them they photographed probably 70 to 80% of the buildings then existing.

They are an interesting part of the social history of Leeds and we believe that images of many of the buildings do not exist elsewhere. Pubs and cinemas traditionally provided a community focal point where local people naturally congregated. All the tram routes had pubs and cinemas particularly in the densely populated areas near to the city centre. There was extensive slum clearance and road improvements in the 1960's and 70's and in the first part of the 21st century a rapid decline in pub numbers because of demographic change, a smoking ban introduced in 2007 and cheap alcohol from supermarkets. The introduction of television resulted in the demise of the cinemas. About 80% of the buildings illustrated have disappeared or are used for other purposes.

Most of the pubs in Leeds were simple humble buildings in working class areas, but there were a few gems that were very ornamental and elaborate. These latter were built in the last decade of the nineteenth and first decade of the twentieth century. To quote Sir John Betjeman, "Leeds burst into a riot of commercial art nouveau".

In 1953 we counted 142 pubs and 34 cinemas on the tram routes in Leeds. These are shown and mostly named on the 1:1250 Ordnance Survey maps published in the 1950's. The earlier 1:2500 maps indicate the larger pubs only. In 2019 thirty five of the pubs we saw in 1953 were still open for business, although some had been rebuilt or renamed. Alas not one cinema remained. Some pubs and beer houses were not shown on the O.S. maps and we apologise if we have missed any. A number of the illustrations have been digitally enhanced.

On some tram routes we have been able to find suitable photographs of all the pubs and cinemas that were seen by the tram passenger, but on some, notably the Dewsbury Road route, we have only found a small number. We have listed and shown on the maps all the pubs and cinemas that were there in 1953, but in the city centre (Briggate, Boar Lane, Duncan Street, Vicar Lane, Kirkgate, and Call Lane) this is more difficult as many pubs adjacent to the tramway were tucked away in yards and not visible to the photographer. Some were residential hotels as opposed to traditional pubs which makes selection difficult. We have therefore not attempted to list these and have included a selection of the more interesting city centre pubs only. These are not included in the counts we made.

In regard to captions, cinema advertisements are well recorded in the local newspapers and acknowledgement must be paid to Robert E. Preedy for his excellent booklet, which lists the Leeds cinemas together with their opening and closure dates and Architects involved. The Brewery History Society has done an excellent job in listing the pubs owned by the various breweries in the Leeds area and this has made the captions much easier to research. They give the dates when the pubs were taken over but unfortunately no closure dates. There is Barry Pepper's "Old Inns and Pubs of Leeds", his book covers the more important inns only and most of the pubs in this L.T.H.S. publication are not mentioned.

There is little in local newspapers about opening, closing or changes of ownership of pubs. However, from the late 1830's to 1890's the annual Brewster Sessions were reported and they give some precise dates.

It was difficult for a publican to obtain a licence as there was much opposition from temperance and religious organisations. There was a complex licensing system and there are details of pub licences granted or revoked, occasional "black" lists, but a lot of pubs sold beer only and were not under the control of the magistrates. Hence they are not mentioned in the Brewster Sessions records. As far as we are aware all the city centre pubs were fully licensed, but in 1953 this was not the case with some suburban pubs. A few individual pubs have been researched by others, existing buildings where deeds and legal documents survive, but most have not. Some had obscure origins as beer houses, brewing their own beer and at first did not have names. The major breweries then became involved, purchasing the beer houses which became "tied houses" selling only the beer supplied by the brewery. The directories give a clue to within a few years when a pub was opened or closed. They are not complete lists, nor are the telephone directories and "yellow pages", but the latter generally give this information to within about a year or two, but, in some cases numbers remained in the directory for three years or more after the building had closed. Pub closures and demolitions are usually unannounced, in some cases publicans doing a "moonlight flit" owing the brewery large sums of money. Exact dates of closure are difficult to find and there are contradictions. Fortunately L.T.H.S. member Tony Wilson whose local, sadly closed in 1977, was the Anchor Inn at Hunslet, and colleague, Malcolm Hargreaves, the local pub historian, have over the past 50 years or so kept observations and noted alterations, closures and demolitions of many of the pubs in this book. We are very grateful for this. We also thank Geoff Williams who gave us access to his vast photograph collection.

Although trams and some buses are featured on almost all the Illustrations the reader will note that there is little mention of them in the captions. Readers are referred to other L.T.H.S. publications for details of rolling stock and tram routes etc.

We hope you enjoy our efforts.

Jim Soper, Leeds Transport Historical Society. June 2019.

# TYMMS HOTEL

The writer had to include Tymms Hotel. It was in Woodhouse Lane very close to the tram route in Cookridge Street and was the hostelry used by students at the adjacent Leeds School of Architecture. At lunchtime we had our sandwiches there with the addition of a Dutton's mild or bitter. Tymms did have a wines and spirits licence, but sold mainly beer.

Tymms was nothing special – a smooth terrazzo floor, nicotine stained walls and ceiling, a plain counter type bar, circular cast iron ornamental tables many years old. The tables had worn and battered oak tops, and there were wooden stools. The landlord was a friendly individual and in cold weather there was a coal fire.

It was a typical working class pub like most of the other pubs illustrated in this book. Tymms terrazzo floor was expensive and "a cut above" most pubs as many still had the traditional black York stone flagged floors. These were common in pubs dating from before about 1910 when muddy macadam roads prevailed. Straw or saw dust was placed on the floor to mop up the mud, dirt, beer spillages – and spit. It kept the floor clean and was swept out daily and a new supply put down the following morning. The writer's maternal grandfather, Richard Atkinson, could recall straw or saw dust being placed on pub floors until the 1914-1918 war. His local was the historic Barley Mow ("Barla Mo" in Richard's Yorkshire dialect) in Bramley Town Street. The Barley Mow was opened by 1830. Sadly it closed suddenly on Saturday, 1 December 2018, and is currently boarded up and for sale. Richard was a character and had an encyclopedic knowledge of Leeds pubs. Directions to any location in Leeds were made by reference to the many locals, e.g. "turn left at the Red Lion, then right at the Black Swan, straight on to the White Horse" etc. etc.

Tymms was a former Albion pub owned by the Albion Brewery, closed in 1933 and on the opposite side of Woodhouse Lane on the site of what is currently the Merrion Centre. The brewery, a plain and depressing looking building, had been bought by Leeds Corporation and demolished about 1937. The site was in use as a car park during the writer's student days. Tymms is recorded in the Albion archive as being opened as a pub by the Brewery in 1925. In 1933 it became a Dutton's pub when that firm bought out Albion.

It was a sad day on Friday, 30 June 1961 when the pub closed and was almost immediately demolished to make way for the new Branch College of Engineering and Science opened in September 1963. The students had a farewell drink with the landlord. The former Leeds School of Architecture building still exists and later became the Leeds College of Music and is currently the Hedley Verity, a J.D. Wetherspoon pub.

The writer although only a "modest" drinker, is interested in the buildings from an architectural and social history view point. He has been responsible for rebuilding at the National Tramway Museum at Crich, Derbyshire, the "High Victorian" Red Lion Hotel from Stoke-on-Trent. It has several art nouveau features.

TYMMS HOTEL, 57 Woodhouse Lane. 1925 – 1961.
Tymms the day after it closed, Saturday, 1 July 1961. The removal van is standing outside.

**PACK HORSE INN, 56 Briggate. By 1613 - date.**
The Pack Horse Inn is stated to be the oldest pub in Leeds. Some say it goes back to the 1130's. The half-timbered building on the left was built in 1613 by Richard Sykes, later an Alderman, and at the side was the entrance to the Pack Horse Yard. The Pack Horse Inn was originally called the Nag's Head and later the Slipin. The 1613 building on the photograph was bought by Timpson's Shoes in 1919 and demolished in 1955 when the firm built a new shop. A Dutton's house, the inn in the yard was removed in 1988 and replaced by a new building.          Date: 3 June 1952.

**WREN'S HOTEL, New Briggate. 1913 – date.**
A view of New Briggate from the top of a tram showing the Wren's Hotel on the left. According to a notice on the building it was "established 1913". It was an Ind Coope and Allsop pub and later a Tetleys' house. It is still in business. The block of property including Rothwell's shop was demolished in December 1967 and January 1968 for Stage 2 of the Inner Ring Road construction.          Date: 4 July 1953.
**TOWER PICTURE HOUSE, New Briggate. 1920 – 1985.**
On the right is the Tower Picture House opened on 12 April 1920 and closed in 1985. It became a night club.

WHIP HOTEL, Between Hirst's Yard, and Bower's Yard, Duncan Street. 1834 - date.
Tucked away between Hirst's Yard and Bower's Yard off Duncan Street and Briggate, the Whip was opened on Tuesday, 6 November 1834, with a "disgusting sign", to quote the Leeds Mercury, of a "coach and horses with the coachman being exhibited in the attitude of begging". The Whip was enlarged in 1883. The photograph was taken on 14 June 1953 and decorations for the Queen's Coronation are still in place. Currently a cocktail bar called Mook, it is still in business.                                                            Date: 14 June 1953.

PEEL HOTEL, 63 Boar Lane. C 1901 - 1967?
The Peel Hotel was on the corner of Bank Street with Boar Lane. In the nineteenth century it was Cowboroughs wine and spirits merchants becoming the Peel Hotel and Restaurant about 1901. According to a report in the Yorkshire Evening Post it was to close at the end of March 1967, but there are reports from other sources that it was open until the late 1970's. About 2013 it was opened as Roxy's Ballroom.                          Date:  26 February 1956.

**ROYAL HOTEL, Briggate. 1692 – 1969-70.**
This building, originally the New Kings Arms, a major Leeds coaching inn, dates from 1692. In 1834 it was renamed the Royal Hotel and rebuilt about the 1890's with a baroque style façade. In 1979 it was demolished and replaced by Regent Court - single person flats. The new building, designed by Architects, Booth Shaw and Partners, has a replica of the baroque facade made of fibreglass. Note the Viaduct Hotel in the background. (see below). Date: 22 July 1956.

**VIADUCT HOTEL, 11 Briggate. C 1880 – date.**
The Viaduct Hotel, was originally a wine and spirit merchant's shop. By 1888 it was called "A Board Vaults" and later Viaduct Vaults. The building still exists and is currently named the Viaduct Showbar. Date: 20 July 1956.

**GOLDEN LION HOTEL, Briggate.  By 1779 - date.**
The Golden Lion Hotel was a former coaching inn dating from before 25 August 1779 when the proprietor Samuel Vincent began running a Diligence to York.  Stage coaches ceased to run from the pub in 1846. In 1878 it was demolished and replaced by the present building the following year. The Architect was Thomas Ambler of Leeds and the hotel opened in early 1880.   In April 2009 it was rebranded the Cosmopolitan and is still in business.
Date:  28 September 1956.

**GENERAL ELLIOTT, 33 Vicar Lane.  By 1807 - date.**
Like all the pubs in Vicar Lane, the General Elliott is an old pub, dating from before 1807. In this photograph, taken on a Sunday morning, it is on the left and behind can be seen the Dolphin, Robin Hood and Nag's Head. (see below). The General Elliott, a traditional Victorian Samuel Smith's pub, until about 1945 formerly owned by Leeds brewer McQuat's, is a grade 2 listed building.
Date: 22 February 1953.

**DOLPHIN HOTEL, 59 Vicar Lane.   By 1817 – C 1960.**
This pub was included in a directory of 1817 and rebuilt in 1902.  It was part of a large complex of lavishly decorated and exuberant buildings, including the Empire Theatre and County Arcade, designed by the leading theatre architect of the day, Frank Matcham, (1854-1920). The buildings were constructed of brick, terra cotta and Burmantofts faience. The Dolphin closed in 1959-1960 and its licence expired on 9 February 1961.          Date: 4 October 1953.

**ROBIN HOOD HOTEL, 71 Vicar Lane.    By 1807 - 1988.**
This was an old pub in existence by 1807.  It was acquired by John Smith's of Tadcaster, rebuilt and reopened in August 1930.  It closed in 1988 and became part of the Duchess of York pub and well known as a music venue.  The Duchess of York closed in 2000 and  was converted into a Hugo Boss shop.          Date:  24 June 1955.

**NAG'S HEAD, 81 Vicar Lane. By 1826 – 2002.**
The Nag's Head was in existence by 1826 and closed in 2002. It was a Tetley's pub and also a free house. The Robin Hood Hotel is the white building to the right of the tram, see above.                                    Date 30 August 1955.

**HOPE INN, North Street/Vicar Lane. By 1846 - 1967.**
On 1 July 1910 a new road, New York Road, connecting North Street with York Road was opened. The Hope Inn and Heaton's Clothing Factory date from this time and are not shown on the 1908 O.S. map. The original Hope Inn dated from the 1840's and was demolished to make way for the new road. The replacement Hope Inn was probably the finest Edwardian pub in Leeds and constructed of terra cotta, faience and tiles. It was taken over by the Albion Brewery, Leeds, in November 1923 and became a Dutton's house in 1933. It remained open until late 1967 and suffered the same fate as its predecessor being bulldozed away in December 1967 and January 1968 when all buildings on the line of Stage 2 of the Inner Ring Road were demolished. Similar buildings are the Garden Gate at Hunslet and the Three Legs on the The Headrow. Heaton's former building on the left still exists.          Date: C 1962.

**MASONS ARMS and REGENT INN, 107 and 109 Kirkgate. By 1817 – C 1952 (Masons Arms), - date Regent.**
These pubs were adjacent to each other and both are listed in a 1817 Directory. In October 1895 the Regent was acquired by Tetley's. The Masons Arms became a Melbourne pub in July 1876 and was later a Tetley's. On the photograph the Masons Arms is dirty and closed and five years or so later other photographs show it as shops. The Regent remains open for business.                                                  Date: 22 February 1953.

**SCOTSMAN, 106 Kirkgate.      By 1882 – C 1992.**
Opposite to the Masons Arms, this pub was taken over from Wallers Bradford Breweries Ltd. by Melbourne in September 1931. A wine merchants in the 1870's, in a 1882 directory it is described as Scotchman Stores. It closed about 1992.                                 Date: 7 November 1959, the last day of tramway operation in Leeds.

9

**STAR AND GARTER 22 Duncan Street . By 1768 – 1981.**
On the corner of Call Lane and Duncan Street, the Star and Garter was a major Leeds coaching inn from 1768 to 1791, the proprietor being a Mr. Strickland. In the twentieth century it was taken over by McQuat's of Leeds and in July 1944 by Samuel Smith's of Tadcaster. It closed as a pub in 1981. The white classical facade to the right of the tram is Hallewell's wine and spirit stores. It later became The Duncan pub which still exists.       Date: 30 August 1953.

**MAJESTIC CINEMA AND NEWS THEATRE, City Square. 1922 - 1969 and 1938 - 1980's.**
The Majestic Cinema dominated City Square and was opened on 5 June 1922, the Architect being Pascal J. Stienlet of Newcastle-upon-Tyne. It closed on 10 July 1969 and was used for bingo, then later became the "Majestyk" night club. The building was damaged by fire and is currently being partially rebuilt. The News Theatre was part of the Queen's Hotel complex and the white vertical motif on the left of the photograph marks its entrance. It was opened on 22 August 1938, became the Classic in 1966, Tatler Film Club in 1969 and the Classic again in 1979. It is currently a night club.     Date: 21 July 1956, the last day of the Tong Road tram services and trams in Boar Lane.

**TATLER CINEMA , Boar Lane. 1915 - 1964.**
The Tatler Cinema was part of the Royal Exchange building (opened 31 August 1875), a decorative Victorian Gothic style structure designed by Thomas Healey. The Tatler's white entrance is on the left of the photograph. It opened as the City Cinema on 4 October 1915, becoming later the Savoy, Academy and then the Tatler News Theatre on 23 December 1936. It closed on 27 January 1964 and the premises were demolished in March and April of that year.
Date: 30 September 1953.

**WEST RIDING HOTEL, 17 Wellington Street. 1857 – date.**
The West Riding Hotel on the right was built in 1857 and given a full licence on 2 September of that year as it was "near to the railway station". The first licensee was Robert Gill. It was taken over by Tetley's Brewery in February 1897 and is still in business.
Date: 4 March 1956.

**ASSEMBLY ROOMS, 32 New Briggate, 1907 - 1985.**
The "miniature theatre" (217 seats), the Assembly Rooms on the right was part of the Grand Theatre complex, designed by Leeds Architect, George Corson (1829-1910), and was opened on 15 April 1907. It changed its name to the Plaza on 25 August 1958 and closed on 14 February 1985. The building is currently called the Howard Assembly Rooms and is used by Opera North.                                                     Date: 1948.

**ODEON CINEMA, 20 The Headrow. 1932 - 2001.**
Opened as the Paramount on 22 February 1932, the facade being designed by Sir Reginald Blomfield, (Architect of The Headrow). The name was changed to the Odeon on 15 April 1940. It opened as a twin cinema on 15 May 1969. After various modifications it closed on 28 October 2001. This photograph was taken on 27 March 1959, the day before the No.3 tram route to Roundhay and Moortown was abandoned.                     Date: 27 March 1959.

# TRAM ROUTE 1, BRIGGATE TO HEADINGLEY AND LAWNSWOOD.

This tram route is unusual as nearly all the pubs that existed in the 1950's are still in business at the time of writing, 2019. This is because of Leeds University and Leeds Beckett University in Woodhouse Lane and the large amount of student residential accommodation in the Headingley area. The students provide the income to keep the pubs in business.

On the section of tram route from City Square to Lawnswood there were ten pubs and one cinema, the Gaumont in Cookridge Street plus two others close to, but not actually on the tram route. These were the Lounge in North Lane and the Headingley Picture House in Cottage Road. The Cottage Road cinema still exists.

From City Square to the start of Woodhouse Lane there were no pubs, the first to be encountered being the Fenton Hotel in Woodhouse Lane, then the Eldon, Packhorse, and Marquis in Woodhouse Lane; the Hyde Park Hotel at the start of Headingley Lane; and in Otley Road the Original Oak, Skyrack, New Inn, Three Horse Shoes and lastly the Woodman Inn at Far Headingley.

As far as we are aware all the pubs on this tram route, apart from the Fenton Hotel, were fully licensed by the 1950's.

The Marquis was demolished to allow for an extension to the University, but the others are still flourishing.

The tram route was abandoned on 3 March 1956.

**THE GAUMONT CINEMA, Cookridge Street. 1905 - 1961.**
Originally named the Coliseum, the building opened on 15 July 1885 as a concert hall and variety theatre. The Architect was William Bakewell (1839-1925) of Leeds. The Coliseum opened as a cinema on 17 April 1905, the first in Leeds, and was taken over by Gaumont Ltd. in the 1930's and on 24 October 1938 renamed the Gaumont-Coliseum. It closed on 23 December 1961 and became a bingo hall. The building still exists and is currently the O2 Academy, a live music venue. 

Date: 30 December 1955.

**FENTON HOTEL, 163 Woodhouse Lane. By 1840 - date.**
The earliest reference we have found to this pub is 24 August 1840 when Anthony Summers unsuccessfully applied to the Justices for a licence for the Fenton Arms. Throughout the tramway period the Fenton sold beer only. According to the firm's records, it has the distinction of being the first pub to be owned by Joshua Tetley & Son Ltd., the eminent Leeds Brewery firm. The premises was acquired in July 1890. It is a typical Victorian three storey brick building and a "modern" 1920's style ceramic tiled front was added to the building later. Being close to the University the pub is popular with students.                Date: 17 September 1955.

**ELDON HOTEL, (formerly CEMETERY TAVERN). 190 Woodhouse Lane. 1834 - date.**
Known as the Cemetery Tavern, this building was opened as a beer house in 1834 and granted a full licence in 1845. On 31 December 1897 it was bought by Tetley's, the name being changed to the Eldon in 1920 after the nearby Eldon Estate. The pub is well patronised and flourishing.                Date: 22 October 1955.

**PACK HORSE INN, 190 later 208 Woodhouse Lane. C 1750 - date.**
The Pack Horse was an old inn. In 1799 it was described as "old and well established" and most probably dated from the mid-eighteenth century. The existing building opened in 1871 and in January 1891 was purchased by Tetley's. The building still displays some of its original internal features and is a popular venue for university students.
Date: 22 October 1955.

**MARQUIS INN, 225 Woodhouse Lane. C 1917 – 1961.**
Originally a beer retailer's premises, by 1917 this building, on the corner of Reservoir Street and Woodhouse Lane, was referred to as the Marquis Inn in local directories. It sold Double Diamond, a popular drink made by Ind Coope & Allsopp Ltd. In 1961 Ind Coope merged with Tetley's to form Allied Breweries. In 1957 and 1961 the property on the right hand side of this photograph was demolished to make way for the Leeds University Engineering Department. The Marquis was in the 1961 batch. The Pack Horse Inn is on the left. Date: 22 October 1955.

**HYDE PARK HOTEL, Headingley Lane, Hyde Park. C 1860 - date.**
Shortly before 1860 the area to the north of Woodhouse Moor became known as Hyde Park. Built on the site of an earlier building, the Hyde Park Hotel originated about this time. It is listed in the census returns of 1861 and latterly was an Ind Coope and Allsop pub. It is still in business.

Date: 3 March 1956, the last day of the Lawnswood tram service.

**THE ORIGINAL OAK INN, 2 Otley Road, Headingley. 18th century – date.**
An old pub, the Original Oak, was named after the adjacent ancient Shire Oak. Eveleigh Bradford in her book about Headingley, states that it was definitely in business as an ale house in 1798, but could date back to at least 1686. In Baines Directory of 1817 it was called the Oak Tree and in 1883 it is recorded as being a Samuel Allsopp pub. In June 1893 it was taken over by Tetley's. It thrives today and is stated to be one of the most successful pubs in the city.

Date: 23 July 1955.

**SKYRACK INN, 2 St.Michael's Road, Headingley. 18th century – date.**
The remarks for the Original Oak Inn above could equally apply to its competitor, the Skyrack, also named after the Shire Oak. Bradford thinks that it was shown on a map dated 1781 and states that it has changed little since it was built over 200 years ago.   It was taken over by the Albion Brewery, Leeds in August 1897 and in 1933 became a Dutton's pub.  The Skyrack is still in business.  The Original Oak is on the right of the photograph.  Date: 23 July 1955.

**NEW INN, 68 Otley Road, Headingley.  By 1841 - date.**
The New Inn is on the corner of Otley Road and Cottage Road and was acquired by Bentley's Yorkshire Breweries on 30 December 1893. In the Directories it is described as an alehouse, but in the 1841 census returns it is stated to be the New Inn, Moor End.   The pub is still in business.                                              Date: 16 July 1955.

17

**THREE HORSE SHOES, 98 Otley Road, Headingley. C 1834 - date.**
The Three Horse Shoes was built in a strategic position at the junction of Otley Road with Addle Road (later Weetwood Lane). It was built by John Askey, a blacksmith, on land he had purchased in July 1832. The Three Horse Shoes was bought by Joshua Tetley & Son in July 1903. The pub is still in business. Note the Woodman Hotel in the background.                                                                                                Date: 5 February 1956.

**WOODMAN HOTEL or INN, 104 Otley Road, Headingley. 1867 -  date.**
Built specifically as a public house in 1866-7, John Farrar was the owner and occupant, unsuccessfully making his first application for a full licence in August 1867. In October 1893 it was acquired by Tetley's, in July 1925 it became a Dutton's pub, and in 1964 a Whitbread house. In the 1970's it was renamed Woodies and after a refit in the 1980's Woodies Ale House. It is still trading. The original stone building had sash windows, but in the twentieth century was "modernised". The windows were changed  and half timbering added to the first floor. Date: 28 November 1953.

# TRAM ROUTE 2, BRIGGATE TO CHAPELTOWN AND MOORTOWN.

For the purposes of this book we have included North Street as part of route 2 although the street was also used by route 3 trams to Harehills and Roundhay and route 6 to Meanwood.

In the 'fifties there were four pubs in North Street, the North Tavern, Golden Lion , White Stag and Eagle Hotel. There was also the Golden Cross Hotel at the bottom of Meanwood Road, which we have included in the Meanwood section. There was The Pointer at Sheepscar and then route 2 itself beginning at the bottom of Chapeltown Road with the Roscoe Inn and then the Cambridge Hotel and Prince of Wales at the junction of Chapeltown Road with Barrack Street and Buslingthorpe Lane. This marked the extent of the densely built up area of Chapeltown Road created in the 1870's. We have also shown the Wellington Inn in Buslingthorpe Lane which could be seen from the Chapeltown tram.

A gap of about 1 1/2 miles separated the Prince of Wales from the Mexborough Arms in Harrogate Road, and then there was the Queen's Arms Hotel at Chapel Allerton and that was it. All were licensed public houses except for the Golden Lion, White Stag, Pointer, Roscoe and Wellington Inn which in the tramway period sold beer only.

Not illustrated here, but about 100 yards from the tramway at Moortown Corner, was the historic uniquely-named Chained Bull pub. It dated from about 1745 and was on the Leeds and Harrogate Turnpike Road. It was rebuilt in 1925, reopening in January 1926. It closed about May 2007 and was demolished in July 2008 becoming a car park for Marks and Spencer.

The White Stag (opened by 1892 and closed early 2008) was situated in Whitelock Street between the Eagle Hotel and the North Tavern. It was visible from the tram but difficult to photograph.

There were three cinemas: The Forum, Dominion and Kingsway, and we also have to mention the Corner House at Moortown Corner which for a short time pre-war was used as a cinema. Of the eleven pubs named in this section only the Mexborough Arms, currently named the Three Hulats, and the Queen's Arms Hotel still exist. The remainder have disappeared as also have the three cinemas. The Corner House building remains although it is now used for other purposes.

Tram route 2 was withdrawn on 28 September 1957.

**NORTH TAVERN, 106 North Street. By 1834 – 1969.**
This building was situated between Darley Street and Byron Passage on North Street and probably dated from the 1890's. Directories show that by 1834 there was a pub of this name on the site. It was taken over by the Melbourne Brewery in 1907 and closed in 1969. It was demolished to make way for the Leeds College of Building.

Date: 28 March 1959, the last day of the Roundhay tram service.

**GOLDEN LION. 95 North Street. 1925-1973.**
Originally a beer retailer's premises, this building between Lovell Road and Lovell Street and to the left of the tram, was taken over by John Smith's of Tadcaster in October 1925 and named the Golden Lion. It closed in June 1973 and was demolished soon afterwards along with other buildings on this part of North Street.　　　Date: 1 June 1957.

**EAGLE HOTEL, 184A North Street. 1832 – date.**
This is the best photograph we have been able to find of a tram passing the Eagle Hotel. It was built in 1826 becoming a beer house in 1832. It was first named the Builder's Inn and had several different names before the Eagle Hotel was adopted. It is a Samuel Smith's pub (ex-McQuat's see page 100) and still in business.
　　　Date: 28 October 1951.

**THE POINTER INN, 84 North Street, later 3 Sheepscar Street South. By 1870 - 2008.**
This inn was a quite impressive building and there was a pub on the site by 1870. The style of architecture suggests that the building on the photograph was probably built about the turn of the century - about 1900. There is photographic evidence to show that it was not there in 1895. It was acquired by John Smith's of Tadcaster from William A. Walker in December 1927. It closed in 2008, the derelict building suffering an arson attack in 2010. The building still stands but has been converted into shops. In tramway days it sold beer only. Date: 1956.

**ROSCOE INN, 11 Chapeltown Road. 1872 - 1982.**
In 1857 a private house built in 1840, and what was to become the Roscoe, was licensed as a beer house. In 1872 it took the name the Roscoe Inn and latterly it became the centre for Irish music in Leeds. In tramway days it was licensed to sell beer only. A Tetley's pub, it closed at midnight on 1 March 1982 and was demolished soon afterwards to make way for the Sheepscar intersection. The Roscoe was replaced by a new pub the New Roscoe, built in Bristol Street nearby. It too closed in January 2017. Date: 5 October 1956.

**BARRACK TAVERN later CAMBRIDGE HOTEL, 56 later 63 and 65 Chapeltown Road. By 1830's – 1969.**
Opened by the early 1830's as the Barrack Tavern, serving the adjacent Cavalry Barracks, the building probably dated from the early 1820's when the barracks were built. In the 1860's it was renamed the Cambridge Hotel. It was purchased by John Smith's of Tadcaster in May 1948. It closed in 1969, was sold to Leeds Corporation in 1970 and demolished not long afterwards.                                                     Date: 8 September 1956.

**PRINCE OF WALES HOTEL, 71 Chapeltown Road. By 1870 - 1982.**
On the northern corner of Buslingthorpe Lane with Chapeltown Road, the Prince of Wales Hotel is listed in directories from 1870. It was taken over by the Albion Brewery, Leeds, in November 1892 and became a Dutton's pub in 1933. The photograph was taken in 1962 and at that time the pub had its original dark green tiled facade. Not long afterwards the tiles were painted brown. The pub closed in January 1982 and was demolished about June or July the same year. Note the Wellington Inn in the background.                                   Date: 23 July 1962.

**WELLINGTON INN, Buslingthorpe Lane. By 1846 – 1970-1.**
Visible from the Chapeltown tram was the Wellington Inn in Buslingthorpe Lane on the corner of Stanhope Terrace. It was a Tetley's pub but is not included in Tetley's lists. The pub is mentioned in a 1846 directory and that is the earliest reference we have. The photograph was taken when slum clearance of the area began and the pub was demolished about 1970-1. The 61/62 East End Park Circular bus service ceased to run along Buslingthorpe Lane from 4 May 1969. This part of Buslingthorpe Lane was closed in the early 1970's.                Date: 23 July 1962.

**THE FORUM CINEMA, Chapeltown Road. 1936 - 1959.**
The Forum was opened on 26 October 1936, the Architect being P.Robinson. It closed on 24 December 1959 and was demolished during February and March 1963. The Forum Garage was built on the site, but it too was subsequently demolished.                Date: 8 September 1956.

**MEXBOROUGH ARMS, 13 Harrogate Road. Early 18th century - date.**

The Mexborough Arms was a very old pub originating in the early eighteenth century and was built on land owned by the Earl of Mexborough. It was on the edge of Chapeltown Moor, where Leeds used to execute its criminals, and figures in accounts of military reviews, horse racing, early cricket matches and sports generally. On 18 June 1774 the 1st battalion of Sir George Savile's West Riding Militia quartered in Leeds "gave an entertainment to officers at Mr. Cowling's, the Mexborough Arms". In its early days it was sometimes called the Bowling Green House, Three Hullats or Savile's Arms. The coat of arms of the Savile family incorporated three owlets, called locally "hullats" or "hulats". In August 1900 it was taken over by Tetley's Brewery, Leeds. In 1924-5 it was replaced by a new building positioned further back from the road. The replacement building on the photograph was opened on 18 November 1925 and reverted to one of its old names, the Three Hulats, in 2006 and it is currently a J.D. Wetherspoon pub.      Date: 1957.

The usual view of the Mexborough Arms from a tram. Being at an angle to Harrogate Road it was difficult to photograph the building with a passing tram.
                                                                                    Date: 29 September 1956.

**THE DOMINION CINEMA, Harrogate Road. 1934 - 1967.**
On the opposite side of the road to the Mexborough Arms was the Dominion Cinema opened on 4 January 1934. The Architect was William Illingworth of Bradford. It was destroyed by fire during the war, but was rebuilt about 1950. It closed on 18 March 1967 and was converted into a bingo hall.        About 25 years later it was demolished.
Date: 2 April 1955.

**THE QUEEN'S ARMS HOTEL, 201 Harrogate Road, C 1841-2 - date.**
The building shown on the photograph dates from 1934 and was a replacement for an earlier Queen's Arms built about 1841-2.  At his third attempt John Cookson was granted its first licence on 26 August 1844.  It was situated on the corner of a new Harrogate Road, opened in 1833, and Woodland Lane.  In December 1894 Joshua Tetley & Son took over the building and sold it in 1933. It still stands today.  The new building was on the opposite side of the road, set back and trees planted along the frontage with Harrogate Road. It was difficult to see and photograph.  The building still exists, the trees have gone and it is currently a Toby Carvery.        Date: 27 April 1957.

**KINGSWAY CINEMA, Harrogate Road. 1937 - 1958.**
The Kingsway opened on 28 June 1937 and had a short life of 19 years closing on 23 August 1958. The Architect was James Brodie of Pudsey. The building opened as the New Vilna Synagogue on 6 September 1959 and was subsequently demolished after a fire in the 1990's.

Date: 28 September 1957, the last day of the Moortown tram service.

**CORNER HOUSE. Moortown Corner. 1938 - 1940.**
The Corner House opened as a cinema on 28 November 1938, the Architect being James Brodie who had been responsible for the Kingsway. Following complaints from the Forum and Kingsway, it closed on 6 January 1940. It became a ballroom and from 1968 to 2008 was a Casino and is currently shops. Date: 28 September 1957.

## TRAM ROUTE 3, BRIGGATE TO HAREHILLS, ROUNDHAY AND MOORTOWN.

In comparison with other routes there were few pubs on this tramway. The section from Sheepscar to Barrack Street was a heavily built up inner city area dating from the 1870's and it supported three pubs: at the Sheepscar end, the Victoria, then the Queen's Hotel on the corner of Roundhay Street, and at Barrack Road the Prince Arthur. For the remaining five miles or so of route to Moortown there were three only: the Fforde Grene at Harehills, the Gipton Hotel near Oakwood and the Deer Park on Street Lane. There were three cinemas, The Gaiety above Spencer Place, and the Harehills Picture House and the Clock both near to each other at Harehills on Roundhay Road. We have also included the Astoria Ballroom on Roundhay Road which when open also served alcoholic drinks. All the pubs on tram route 3 were fully licensed as public houses.

The Gipton Hotel, currently named The Roundhay, and Deer Park are still in business, but the other pubs have gone.

The buildings, formerly the Victoria Inn, Fforde Grene and Clock Cinema, are extant but used for other purposes.

The tram route was abandoned on 28 March 1959.

**VICTORIA INN, 4, later 8 Roundhay Road, Sheepscar. By 1870 – 2016.**
The Victoria Inn is referred to in a Directory of 1870 and was probably built soon after 1867 when tolls on the Leeds and Roundhay Turnpike Road, or Roundhay Road, were removed and the area became developed. It was formerly owned by Rilot's Brewery and was purchased by Tetley's in December 1926 and closed at the end of December 2016. The building still stands and is currently used as a community centre for a Hindu charitable organisation.
Date: 17 January 1954.

**QUEEN'S HOTEL , 23, later 27 later 54 Roundhay Road. By 1841 - 1966.**
On the corner of Roundhay Street, this pub was built about 1840-1 and at his third attempt on 28 August 1843 William Craister was granted its first licence. It served the nearby Cavalry Barracks situated between Chapeltown Road and Roundhay Road. It appears to have been rebuilt about 1900 in a Georgian/Victorian style with a tiled ground floor and white faience upper floors. It was acquired by John Smith's of Tadcaster in January 1919 and sold to Leeds Corporation in 1967. It closed in 1966 and was demolished not long afterwards.     Date : 28 March 1959.

**PRINCE ARTHUR HOTEL, 53 later 71 Roundhay Road. By 1873 – C 1997.**
Between Boundary Street and Boundary Place, this pub was built by 1873 when James Sadler, formerly of the Hope Inn, unsuccessfully applied for its first licence. By 1953 it was fully licensed. It was latterly owned by Ind Coope then Tetley's and closed about 1997. It was demolished about 2005.     Date: 16 September 1958.

**GAIETY CINEMA, Roundhay Road. 1921 – 1958.**
The Gaiety Cinema opened on 6 July 1921 and closed on 22 February 1958.  The style was typical of the early 1920's and it was built of brick and faience.  The Architect was G.F. Bowman of Leeds.  It was demolished in August and September 1970 and a pub, also named the Gaiety, built on the site.  The pub opened on 7 December 1972, but due to drug and vandalism problems was closed and then demolished in November and December 1997.

Date: 28 March 1959, the last day of the Roundhay tram service.

**THE PICTURE HOUSE, HAREHILLS, 250 Roundhay Road. 1912 - 1963.**
The Harehills Picture House opened on 16 December 1912 and closed on 5 October 1963.  The Architect was W.P.Schofield of Leeds.  Bingo started on 11 October 1963, but was short lived.  The building was demolished in July 1968 to make way for a supermarket.

Date: 27 September 1958.

29

**FFORDE GRENE HOTEL, Harehills. 1938 – 2004.**
This is the best picture we have been able to find of the Fforde Grene with a tram. The pub is to the right of the tram. The Fforde Grene opened at 5.30 pm on 25 November 1938, the Architects being Pennington, Hustler and Taylor of Leeds. E.V. Ford was the Managing Director of the Melbourne Brewery and the pub name came from the family estate in Staffordshire called Fforde Grene. The pub closed abruptly on Thursday 15 July 2004 following a drugs raid in which 26 people were arrested. Three years later it became a supermarket. Date 1959.

**CLOCK CINEMA, Roundhay Road, Harehills. 1938 - 1976.**
The Clock opened on 21 November 1938 and closed on 28 February 1976. It reopened for Mecca bingo, and is now an electrical warehouse. The Architects were Kitson, Parish, Ledgard and Pyman of Leeds. Date: 27 September 1958.

**CLOCK CINEMA.**
A view looking up Easterly Road showing the Clock Cinema two months after it closed.  There is a large "For sale or to let" sign on the building.                                    Date:  8 May 1976.

**ASTORIA BALLROOM, Roundhay Road, Harehills.  1929 - 1992.**
The Astoria was opened as the Harehills Palais de danse in 1929 and was later renamed the Astoria.  It closed in 1992 and was used as Amriks electrical store until 1996 when it closed following a fire.  It was then demolished and replaced with flats.                                    Date: 27 September 1958.

**GIPTON HOTEL, 605 Roundhay Road. 1842 – date.**
It was virtually impossible to photograph a tram passing the Gipton Hotel in Roundhay Road because the building was set back from the road. The best picture we have found shows the pub sign only. The present building, currently named The Roundhay, is a replacement for an earlier building sited much nearer to Roundhay Road. The original pub was built about 1840 and first licensed to Jonathon Alderson on 29 August 1842.          Date: 4 October 1958.

**DEER PARK, 68 Street Lane, Roundhay. C 1938 - date.**
The mock tudor Deer Park Hotel was built shortly before the Second World War by Tetley's and is still in business.
                                                                Date: 28 March 1959.

# TRAM ROUTE 4,   BRIGGATE TO KIRKSTALL ABBEY.

For the purposes of this book we are covering the section of route 4 from Wellington Bridge to the terminus. The area from Wellington Bridge to Burley Mills was heavily built up with working class housing, densely populated and hence could support a lot of pubs. There was then a semi-rural section to Kirkstall village, again with a substantial population and more pubs.  In 1953 there were two cinemas on the route, the Abbey Cinema in Abbey Road, Kirkstall, and Embassy (formerly the Atlas) -1 May 1912 - 17 November 1956 - at 281 Kirkstall Road.   There were also two closed cinemas, the Wellington (1920 – 1941) at 226 Wellington Street, and the Imperial (1913 – 1940) at 79 Kirkstall Road.

On the short section of Wellington Street which marks the start of this section there were two pubs,  the Wellington and the Junction Inn, the latter on the junction with West Street. Proceeding up Kirkstall Road there were the Woolpack, Morning Star, New Inn, Rising Sun, Milford Inn and Cardigan Arms.  On Commercial Road in Kirkstall village there were the Woodman, Old George, George IV and Royal Sovereign.  In Abbey Road there was West End House.  All the pubs were on the north side of the tram route except for the Milford Inn which was directly opposite the Rising Sun.  There was a total of 13 pubs of which only two, the Cardigan Arms  and West End House are still in business.  The derelict shells of the Rising Sun and George IV are still extant.

There was and still exists the Vesper Gate pub a few hundred yards beyond Kirkstall Abbey.  This was on the Hawksworth Road section of tram route abandoned in 1949 and outside the remit of this book.

During the tramway period the Morning Star, New Inn, Woodman and George IV  were licensed to sell beer only.

In the 1950's the city end of KIrkstall Road was a rather depressing area.  On the south side were industrial buildings and on the north dereliction.  There were a number of cleared areas and boarded up buildings and it was not attractive to photographers.  The Woolpack (opened by 1828, rebuilt 1878-1879, closed 1972) and Morning Star (closed 1970), were there, but we have been unable to find any photographs.

Tram route 4 ceased running on 3 April 1954, the section from Kirkstall Road tramway works to City Square remained open until 1957.

**WELLINGTON INN, 195 later 202 Wellington Street.  By 1839 - 1971.**
The Wellington Inn was an old inn and the earliest reference we have found is in a directory of 1839.  The original building was demolished in 1866 and replaced the following year by the building on the photograph.  It was taken over by John Smith's of Tadcaster in August 1896.  The pub closed in May 1971 and the building was demolished to make way for the approaches to the new Inner Ring Road.                                              Date: 15 April 1956.

33

**JUNCTION INN, 163 West Street. By 1839 - 1972.**
The Junction Inn was on the corner of Wellington Street and West Street at its junction with Kirkstall Road. It dominated the junction and was in existence as a beer house by 1839. On 31 August 1846 it was fully licensed by the magistrates, the first licensee being William Fleming. Latterly the pub was owned by Samuel Smith's of Tadcaster. It remained open until early 1972 when it and all the property on the east side of this part of Wellington Street, including the Wellington Inn, visible in the distance, were cleared for Stage 3 of the Inner Ring Road.
The front of the former Wellington Picture House is just to the right of the tram. It opened on 9 November 1920 and closed on 5 November 1941. It became a warehouse and was demolished in 1972.                    Date: 3 April 1954.

**IND COOPE AND ALLSOPP LTD. OFFICES AND STORES, 18 Kirkstall Road. 19th century - C 1972.**
Between Wortley Street and Wellington Terrace, this building was formerly the registered office of the Leeds City Brewery Ltd. It was four doors away from 26 Kirkstall Road, the Woolpack Inn, and by 1936 was the Leeds office of the major Burton-on-Trent brewery company Ind Coope & Allsopp Ltd. Behind the building was a beer bottling store. Note in the misty background, the Junction Inn above. About 1972 the buildings on this part of Kirkstall Road were demolished.                    Date: 24 January 1954.

**NEW INN, 228 Kirkstall Road. 1847- 1970.**
Built in 1847 the New Inn was on the corner of Kirkstall Road and Willow Road "near Messrs. Whithams foundry", and was a typical almost standard design nineteenth century working class beer house. The first owner was David Thornton and in December 1881 it was acquired by John Smith's of Tadcaster. It closed in 1970 and was demolished to make way for the widening of Kirkstall Road and Willow Road.                    **Date: 1 April 1954.**

**RISING SUN INN, 290 Kirkstall Road. By 1880 – 2009.  MILFORD INN,  243 Kirkstall Road. By 1870 – 1973.**
Just behind the tram on the left is the Rising Sun Inn, a Melbourne house, and on the right the Milford Inn at 243 Kirkstall Road which sold Dutton's Ales. The pub was purchased by the Melbourne Brewery in 1896 and a new building was designed by Architect Thomas Winn of Albion Street, Leeds, in 1899.  A licence had been granted on 30 September 1898. It opened about 1900 and has a very fine interior with high ceilings and is Grade 2 listed. The pub closed in July 2009 and in 2011 was a shop selling second hand furniture.  It suffered fire damage in 2013 and flood damage on Boxing Day 2015 and is currently derelict.  The much more modest Milford Inn was built by 1870 and closed in 1973.                    **Date: 11 July 1953.**

**RISING SUN INN.**
A 1986 photograph of the Rising Sun Inn. The vacant site formerly occupied by the Milford Inn is on the right.

Date: 8 September 1986.

**CARDIGAN ARMS. 364 Kirkstall Road.   C 1802 – date.**
The Cardigan Arms is an old pub dating from the first decade of the nineteenth century and was a staging post on the new turnpike road from Kirkstall to Leeds opened in 1802. From 1834 to 1861 there was a toll gate at this point. The present building is not the original, but a replacement built in 1896, the Architect being Thomas Winn who also designed its competitor the Rising Sun. It too is a fine example of the exuberant architectural style of the 1890's. Tetley's took over the building in July 1927. The Cardigan Arms is still in business and has been restored by the new Kirkstall Brewery.

Date: 16 January 1954.

**WOODMAN INN, 95 Commercial Road, Kirkstall. By 1834 – C 1966.**
The Woodman was an old beer house and there was a pub on the site by 1834. It was taken over by Melbourne in October 1895. It seems likely that the mock tudor building was built by Melbourne as a replacement building. The Woodman is listed in a directory of 1962, and closed about 1966.                    Date: 27 March 1954.

**GEORGE HOTEL, 91 Commercial Road, Kirkstall. By 1834 – 1966.**
The companion Inn to the Woodman, the George Hotel, was also in existence by 1834. Probably because of its age it had a full licence. In its early days it was owned by the Kirkstall Brewery, but became a Dutton's house when that firm took over the Kirkstall Brewery in 1936. It closed in 1966 about the same time as the Woodman.
                                        Date: 21 December 1952.

**GEORGE HOTEL.**
The George Hotel from the opposite direction looking towards Leeds with the Woodman Inn behind. The George had an unfair advantage over its neighbours the Woodman and George IV. It was fully licensed whereas they were allowed to sell beer only.                                                    Date: 27 March 1954.

**GEORGE IV, 59 Commercial Road, Kirkstall. 1896 – 2006.**
We have been unable to find any reference to the George IV until June 1896 when it was acquired by Tetley's. It was built in a classical opulent style of the 1890's and we assume it was built by Tetley's. In tramway days it sold beer only. It was refurbished in 2001 but closed in 2006 although the telephone apparently remained connected until 2009. It was advertised for sale on 1 January 2010. Like the Rising Sun and Cardigan Arms it is a listed building. It is currently derelict.                                                    Date: 11 October 1953.

**ROYAL SOVEREIGN, 19 Commercial Road., Kirkstall.    1839 - 1976.**
This pub was unusual as it was built sideways to Commercial Road, the entrance being in Sovereign Yard. It was at the heart of the old Kirkstall village, sacrificed to the motor car in the 1970's when the old stone buildings on the photograph were demolished. It was also unusual for a suburban pub to advertise its opening, but on 20 April 1839 an advertisement appeared in the Leeds Mercury. The pub closed in December 1976.        Date: 11 October 1953.

**WEST END HOUSE, 26 Abbey Road, Kirkstall. 1867 – date.**
This building was first listed as a beer house in 1867, but by 1870 was referred to as West End House, the first licensee being William Tordoff. He gave his name to several streets in the surrounding area. The Kirkstall Brewery supplied beer from 1867 to 1936 when Duttons' took over and the pub is still in business. The Abbey Cinema is on the left.                                                Date: 7 July 1953.

**WEST END HOUSE**
After the buildings on the right had been removed, Dutton's West End House looking towards Kirkstall Abbey. The Former Abbey Cinema (see below) is in use as a Bingo Hall.                                        Date: 7 October 1967.

**ABBEY PICTURE HOUSE, 30 Abbey Road, Kirkstall. 1913 - 1960.**
This cinema opened on 22 September 1913, the Architect being Fred Mitchell. It closed on 8 October 1960 and was initially used for bingo. The building still stands.                                        Date: 11 October 1953.

# TRAM ROUTE 5, CORN EXCHANGE TO BEESTON AND ROUTE 8, CORN EXCHANGE TO ELLAND ROAD.

Meadow Lane was used by several services and we are including it under route 9 to Dewsbury Road. This section covers Meadow Road used by both the Beeston and Elland Road trams.  We have placed the White House pub at the bottom of Dewsbury Road in the route 9 section.  On Meadow Road there was only one pub, the Royal Oak, on the corner of Jack Lane plus a malt house used by Tetley's Brewery called Meadow Maltings, the entrance to which is illustrated. There was the large pub, the Coach and Horses at the junction of Meadow Road with Beeston Road and Elland Road and the Queen's Theatre and Palace Cinema on Meadow  Road.

On the Beeston tram route there were two cinemas,  the Malvern and the Picture Theatre at 13 Town Street near Old Lane, and four pubs: the Old Golden Lion Hotel and the Duke of York Hotel in Beeston Road and the Old White Hart and Punch Bowl in Town Street, Beeston.

As far as we are aware all the pubs on both the Beeston and Elland Road routes were fully licensed in the tramway era.

On 15 December 1972 a 2½ mile extension of the M1 motorway was formally opened through to Leeds  and  many of the  roads used by the former tramways covered in this section disappeared.  They were Meadow Road, most of Meadow Lane, the lower part of Dewsbury Road and the lower part of Beeston Road.  All the buildings on the line of route were demolished during 1971 including the White House Hotel and Union Tavern (both covered under routes 9 and 12),  Meadow Maltings, Royal Oak and the Coach and Horses.  Much of the former Elland Road tramway disappeared about two years later to be replaced by the M621 Motorway.

The Old Golden Lion Hotel, the Old White Hart, the Old Peacock, in rebuilt form, and the Waggon and Horses, renamed the United Bar, still exist.   We have been unable to find a suitable photograph of the Picture Theatre.

The Elland Road tram route ceased operation on 25 June 1955.  On 19 November 1955 the last tram ran on route 5 to Beeston.

**ROYAL OAK, 48 Meadow Road,   1820's – C 1969.**
At the Brewster Sessions in August 1853 it was stated that there had been a beer house on this site from the 1820's. In 1853 Benjamin Hargrave was the owner.  The building on the photograph probably dates from about April 1926 when Tetley's took over the pub. It was a typical 1920's building and was almost certainly built by Tetley's.  It was demolished in 1970-1971, along with everything else on Meadow Road, to make way for Motorway construction.
Date: 17 October 1955.

41

**MEADOW MALTINGS, Meadow Road. 1880's – C 1968.**
The Meadow Maltings was not a pub but a malt house on Meadow Road used by brewers Joshua Tetley & Son Ltd. By the late 1880's a Joshua Robinson had opened a malt house and this was later taken over by Tetley's. Note the Guy lorry on the right, registration number NNW 894, owned by the Melbourne Brewery. Leeds.    Date: 17 October 1955.

**QUEEN'S PICTURE THEATRE, Meadow Road. 1898 - 1957.**
The Queens Theatre, on the corner of Meadow Road and Jack Lane, was a large building and opened as a theatre on 26 December 1898. The Architects were Hope and Maxwell of Newcastle. Its last stage performance was on 17 July 1924. It reopened as a cinema on 1 December 1924 and closed on 19 October 1957. It was demolished in February and March 1968.                                                                    Date: 15 November 1955.

**COACH AND HORSES 2 Beeston Road, 1 Elland Road. By 1834 - 1972.**
The Coach and Horses was in a prominent position at the junction of Meadow Road with Beeston Road and Elland Road and was a splendid Edwardian hotel opened by John Smith's Brewery in October 1909. It was built on the site of another pub which had been in existence by 1834, but was probably earlier. The Coach and Horses was closed in either November or December 1972 and demolished soon afterwards.                    Date: 15 November 1955.

**OLD GOLDEN LION HOTEL, 42 Beeston Road. By 1853 – date.**
Very close to the M621 Motorway this fine building survived the wholesale demolition of 1972-3. It was an Ind Coope and Allsopp house and was a product of the Victorian/Edwardian 1890-1910 decorative period, close to and in competition with the Coach and Horses. We have been unable to find the exact year it was built, but it was on the site of an earlier pub in existence by 1853. The pub is still in business.                    Date: 16 August 1955.

**DUKE OF YORK, Beeston Road.  By 1834-1974.**
Situated at the bottom of Beeston Hill not far from the Old Golden Lion Hotel, the Duke of York was an old pub and is listed in an 1834 directory.  It was taken over by Tetley's in February 1896 but became a  John Smith's of Tadcaster pub in May 1928.   The pub closed in 1974.                                    Date: 12 November 1955.

**MALVERN  PICTURE PALACE, 82-86 Beeston Road. 1912-1971.**
This cinema opened on 23 December 1912 and closed on 28 August 1971.  The Architect was W.E. Beevers of Leeds. It was used as a bingo hall for a number of years, became derelict and was demolished.  A new pub called the Malvern was built on the site, but it closed in 2008 and was subsequently demolished.          Date: 24 October 1955.

**MALVERN PICTURE PALACE.**
A view of the Malvern Picture Palace looking towards Beeston.                    Date: 24 October 1955.

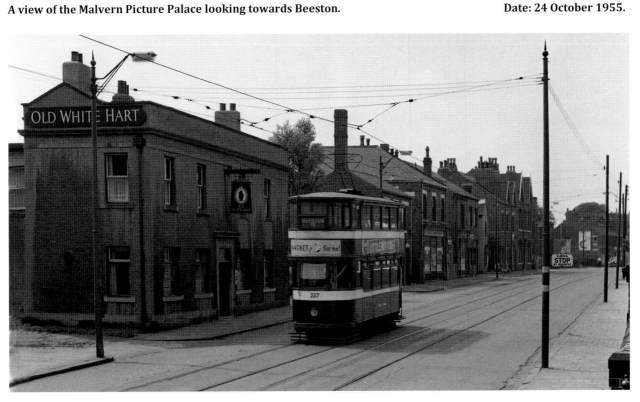

**OLD WHITE HART, 45 Town Street, Beeston.  By 1826 - date.**
The Old White Hart was bought from Ind Coope by Tetley's in March 1960.  In the 1920's it was owned by the Leeds City Brewery.  It was an old pub and listed in a 1826 directory.   It is near to the football ground, well patronised by Leeds United fans and is still in business. On the photograph the Punch Bowl pub can be seen in the distance to the left of the tram stop sign.                    Date: 15 August 1955.

**OLD PUNCH BOWL, Town Street, Beeston. By 1826 to 1977.**
Close to the Old White Hart, the Old Punch Bowl was also an elderly pub and listed in the same 1826 directory as its neighbour, the Old White Hart. It is stated to have been rebuilt in the 1890's and became a Melbourne pub in May 1920 and in 1960 a Tetley's. It closed in 1977. Date: 20 September 1955.

**WAGGON AND HORSES, 82 Elland Road. 1820's – date.**
Another old pub dating from soon after the opening of the turnpike road in 1824. It was built as a resting place for travellers and was in open countryside at the time. Originally owned by the Leeds City Brewery it was later an Ind Coope pub and closed in early 2008. It reopened for Leeds United fans as the United Bar in January 2010, but closed again after a short period. It reopened again and is still in business. Date: 18 June 1955.

**WAGGON AND HORSES.**
Passengers waiting to board the Meanwood tram at the Waggon and Horses tram stop, Elland Road.  At this point there is currently a deep cutting for the M621 Motorway.                                              Date:  22 June 1955.

**NEW PEACOCK INN, 142 Elland Road, 1838 - 1974.**
The New Peacock Inn was built in 1838 by William Bradley the former tenant of the Peacock Inn some 300 yards to the south west.  Licensed as the Prince George on 1 September 1840 it was renamed the New Peacock Inn the following month.  It was taken over by Bentley's Yorkshire Breweries Ltd. in May 1876.  This part of Elland Road was closed to through traffic in January 1975. The New Peacock Inn closed in May 1974 and was demolished in October 1975 to allow the construction of an approach road to the new M621 motorway.                    Date: 18 June 1955.

**OLD PEACOCK, Elland Road. By 1826 - date.**
This pub is opposite the Leeds United Football Ground in Elland Road. It is an old pub and first appears in a directory of 1826. Originally named the Peacock, it became the Old Peacock some years after the New Peacock opened. In May 1892 it was purchased by Richard Whitaker & Sons, brewers of Halifax and a year later was sold to Bentley's Yorkshire Breweries. It was rebuilt in 1963 and moved further back from Elland Road and resited more to the east. It is still in business and is currently owned by the Ossett Brewery. It had a major refit in 2013.

Date: 18 June 1955.

**OLD PEACOCK.**
The Old Peacock looking towards the Greyhound Stadium and Morley.

Date 22 June 1955.

# TRAM ROUTE 6, CORN EXCHANGE TO MEANWOOD.

At the Sheepscar end of North Street the Meanwood tram route joined the 2 and 3 tram routes to Moortown and Roundhay. At North Street was the Golden Cross junction, dominated by the Golden Cross Hotel. The Sheepscar part of the tramway was very densely populated with working class back to back housing. Meanwood Road was lined with corner shops and a sprinkling of pubs on either side. It was a very busy and vibrant place in which to live.

The "Leeds, Woodhouse Carr and Meanwoodside Road", or Meanwood Road was a former turnpike road opened in 1831 and had been acquired by Leeds Corporation in 1866. Soon afterwards, the area became rapidly built up between Sheepscar and Woodhouse Carr.

In the later tramway days between the Golden Cross and Woodhouse Carr, i.e. the corner of Buslingthorpe Lane, there were seven pubs: The Old Toll Bar, near Crimbles Street; the Kings Arms on the southern corner of Meanwood Street; the New Inn just above Barrack Street; the Globe Inn on the northern corner of Sackville Street; the Oak Inn on the corner of Horrock Street, opposite the Junction Hotel on the corner of Buslingthorpe Green, and the Primrose Hotel at Buslingthorpe Lane. There was an off licence on the corner of Cambridge Road. This was extent of the built up area of Meanwood Road and the Primrose Hotel had been the terminus of the former horse tram route. There were fewer buildings north west of the Primrose. There were two cinemas: the Capitol Cinema and Ballroom near the tram terminus, and a small cinema called the Royal near the Globe Inn and opposite Oatland Road. An earlier cinema, the Golden Cross Electric Theatre, had existed from 1910 to 1925. There were two more pubs: the Meanwood Hotel (known colloquially as "The Melbourne") at the junction with Grove Lane and the Beckett's Arms at the tram terminus. Of the pubs, the New Inn, Globe, Oak and Junction were beer houses selling beer only.

We have not been able to find any photographs of the Oak Inn which was closed about 1971-2. At the time of writing, 2019, there are no cinemas and only one pub, The Primrose, remaining on the former tram route.

The tram route closed on 25 June 1955.

**GOLDEN CROSS HOTEL, 63, later 191 North Street, Sheepscar. By 1837 – 1969.**
The Golden Cross Hotel and Midland Bank dominated the junction of Meanwood Road with North Street. The Golden Cross was an old pub built by 1837 not long after the opening of the Turnpike Road. It had its own brew house and was taken over by Bentley's Yorkshire Breweries in 1913. It was a simple white painted brick building with a classical style extension with bay windows to the ground floor probably added by Bentleys. By the mid-'sixties, because of slum clearance, it was an isolated building. In 1968 it found itself on the edge of a section of phase 2 of the Inner Ring Road works, an extension of Claypit Lane to Sheepscar, and closed in December 1969 under a compulsory purchase order by Leeds Corporation. It was boarded up and demolished in early 1970. The former Midland Bank building on the right, a listed building, still exists. The tram is advertising Hemingway's Noted Ales. (see page 82). Date: 5 June 1955.

**EAGLE HOTEL.**
The Golden Cross junction with a good view of North Street taken from the Midland Bank corner, (see previous page). In the middle distance is the Eagle Hotel in North Street. The Golden Cross Hotel is opposite the tram but out of sight. The photograph was taken on the last day of the Meanwood tramway.      Date: 25 June 1955.

**GOLDEN CROSS HOTEL.**
About 40 to 50 yards from the previous photograph and looking down Meanwood Road to North Street with the north east side of the Golden Cross Hotel on the right.      Date: 19 June 1955.

**THE OLD TOLL BAR, 19 Meanwood Road.  By 1868- 1962.**
The Old Toll Bar was a small simple painted brick building just over 100 yards from the Golden Cross.  It was to the north west of Crimbles Street and close to the old Crimbles Bar, the toll bar at the start of the turnpike road.    The pub was taken over by the Melbourne Brewery in October 1920.  The first landlord was Joseph Foster and in 1872 it appeared on a "black list" of pubs.  It was presumably part of the original toll bar, which had closed on 1 January 1867, or possibly a new building built on or very near the site of the bar. It was still in business in October 1961, but disappeared the following year when much of the property on the west side of Meanwood Road from Sheepscar to Oatland Road was demolished.                                                                                       Date: 25 June 1955.

**THE KINGS ARMS, 73 Meanwood Road.  C 1834 – 1971.**
Because of traffic congestion Keith Terry had a struggle to photograph The Kings Arms in 1955.  The Kings Arms was a Tetley's pub acquired in October 1906.  It occupied the site of an earlier pub which had existed by 1834 soon after the turnpike had opened.  The second building  appears to have been a replacement pub built by Tetley's.  When the property on the south west side of Meanwood Road was demolished in 1962 the pub stood in isolation for about ten years and was closed and demolished following a fire in March 1971.  A replacement pub, the New Kings Arms, opened on 25 June 1971, but it too was subsequently demolished in 1999.                                           Date: 23 June 1955.

## THE KINGS ARMS.

When this photograph was taken the Kings Arms was an isolated building on the south west side of Meanwood Road. The Meanwood Stores on the left on the corner of Barrack Street are closed and awaiting demolition. Nearly all the property between Barrack Street and Sackville Street had gone, but the New Inn, almost opposite the bus stop, and illustrated below, and the shops on each side, were still clinging on.                    Date 2 September 1967.

## NEW INN, 76 Meanwood Road. 1843 – 1970.

Situated between Barrack Street and Wilmington Street, the tiny beer house, the New Inn was built by 1843 and acquired by the Melbourne Brewery in April 1925. In 1843 the first landlord was June Wilson who repeatedly and unsuccessfully tried to obtain a full licence over the following years. Between about June and October 1965, in a slum clearance programme, the property to the north of Meanwood Road between Barrack Street and Sackville Street was demolished and the area fenced off. This included the Wilmingtons, but the New Inn and the shops at either side of it lasted until 1970. It was probably something to do with the pub's lease.                    Date: 23 June 1955.

**THE GLOBE INN, 116 Meanwood Road. 1921 – C 2000.**
This pub is the only one on the lower part of Meanwood Road which escaped demolition in the 1960's and 70's. It was on the north west corner of Meanwood Road at Sackville Street and was formerly a beer seller's premises. John Smith's of Tadcaster built a new pub on the site which it called the Globe Inn. It had its own brewhouse and opened in December 1921. It closed about 2000. In 2007 it was converted into four flats the frontage to Meanwood Road being replaced by a boring blank white painted wall. In tramway days the Globe sold beer only. Date: 23 June 1955.

**ROYAL CINEMA, 136 Meanwood Road. 1913 - 1966.**
The Royal Cinema is the white building with three upper windows on the left of this photograph. It was opened as the Atlas Picture House on 8 October 1913 and renamed the Royal on 3 April 1935. It was opposite Oatland Road and a few doors above the Globe Inn which is to the left of the tram. The disappearance of its custom – the people in the houses in the immediate area - led to its closure on 29 October 1966. The premises were acquired by Kingfisher Lubrication Ltd., but later demolished. Date: 23 June 1955.

**JUNCTION HOTEL, 82 later 240 Meanwood Road. By 1865– C 1971-2.**
This beer house to the right of the tram, was situated on the corner of Buslingthorpe Green with Meanwood Road and was latterly a Dutton's pub, opened by 1865 and closed about 1971-2. In 1866 it was described as a "well conducted beer house" and the landlord was John Wood. The O.S. map shows that on the opposite side of Meanwood Road there was another beer house, the Oak Inn, but we have not seen any photographs.          Date: 9 June 1955.

**THE PRIMROSE HOTEL, Meanwood Road. 1887 - date.**
The Primrose Hotel on the corner of Buslingthorpe Lane is the only pub on the former Meanwood tram route which still exists. A beer house was opened in 1860 and replaced by the present building opened on 25 August 1887. The first landlord was Frederick Rainsford Dawson. He had received a full licence in September 1886 when the drawings were submitted to the Licensing Magistrates. The pub was the terminus for the Meanwood horse tram route from 1878. It was leased to John Smith's of Tadcaster in March 1908 and taken over by the firm in April 1927. This view was taken at the tram stop on 19 June 1955. The "Goodness Me" OXO advert was common place and popular at the time.                                                                          Date 19 June 1955.

**THE PRIMROSE HOTEL.**
A more panoramic view of the Primrose taken from the west side of Meanwood Road. The large chimney to the front corner of the building has been taken down and the premises is currently a free house.     Date: 21 June 1955.

**THE MEANWOOD HOTEL, junction of Grove Lane with Meanwood Road. 1927 – C 2002.**
The Meanwood Hotel was a long symmetrical building and the best picture we have been able to find shows the left half of the building only. In comparison with the other pubs on the Meanwood tram route, it was a modern building licensed and opened on 26 July 1927, the licence being transferred from the Smithfield Hotel in North Street which had lapsed in 1925. It was built to serve the new Meanwood Housing Estate.   The Meanwood Hotel closed about 2002, was demolished and replaced with flats.     Date: 21 June 1955.

**BECKETT'S ARMS, Meanwood.   By 1834 - 2005.**
The art deco style building was built in 1938 and was a replacement for an earlier building of which the early history is obscure. By 1834 there was an inn on the site named the Dusty Miller, but by 1839 was referred to as the Beckett's Arms.  In October 1896 it was sold to John Smith's of Tadcaster.  The new building opened on 9 February 1939 and the old demolished almost immediately afterwards.  The replacement building ceased to trade in 2005 and was demolished in April and May 2007.                                                   Date: 25 June 1955.

**THE CAPITOL CINEMA AND BALLROOM, Green Road, Meanwood.  1922 – 1968.**
 If you look carefully you can just see a tram standing at the terminus on the last day of tramway operation, 25 June 1955.  The photograph was taken to show the new bus stop outside the Capitol Cinema.  The cinema was opened on 27 November 1922, closed on 27 July 1968 and a month later the ballroom closed.  The cinema was used for a Mecca Bingo and the ballroom a disco.  The premises were demolished in 1980.                  Date:  25 June 1955.

# TRAM ROUTES 9, CORN EXCHANGE OR BRIGGATE TO DEWSBURY ROAD. 10, CORN EXCHANGE TO COMPTON ROAD. 11, CORN EXCHANGE TO GIPTON ESTATE AND 12, SWINEGATE TO MIDDLETON.

In this section we are covering Meadow Lane from Bridge End to Meadow Road, Dewsbury Road, Moor Road, the Middleton Light Railway and the short sections of tramway route to Compton Road and the Gipton Estate.

In 1953 there were some very old pubs in Meadow Lane beginning with the Old Red Lion on the corner at Bridge End; the Old George, Red House, Jacob's Well, Union Tavern and the White House at the junction of Meadow Lane, Meadow Road and Dewsbury Road. The lower part of Dewsbury Road was industrialised and run down with some slum housing. It had seven pubs: the Parkfield Hotel (opened by 1858) on the corner of Jack Lane followed by the Cricketer's Arms; the Sir Robert Peel and Silver Cross Inn (opened by 1858, licence granted 30 August 1861) opposite each other at Silver Cross Street; the Beulah Inn (opened by 1883, licence granted 25 August 1887) on the corner of Bewerley Street; the King's Arms, and the Junction Hotel, on the corner of Moor Road and Dewsbury Road. This was where tram route 12 to Middleton branched off. Above the Junction Hotel on Dewsbury Road was the Green Man Inn on the corner of Vicar Street, the New Inn, Broadway and the Tommy Wass Hotel at the terminus. Just visible from the tram terminus was the Rex Cinema on the Ring Road Beeston Park. Lower down Dewsbury Road were the Pavilion Cinema on the corner of Rowland Road and Crescent Cinema at Garnet Road. Unfortunately Meadow Lane and the lower part of Dewsbury Road were not attractive to photographers, few photographs were taken and we have been unable to find many pictures of the pubs in this area which are good enough for publication. The Sir Robert Peel closed on 30 September 1966 and the others were demolished about 1968-9 to make way for the M1 extension through to Meadow Lane. The Old Red Lion, Broadway and Tommy Wass Hotel are still in business. The Junction Hotel, now used as flats, and the New Inn, an Asian supermarket, still exist.

On Moor Road, the start of route 12, there was the Moor House Inn which still exists and the Middleton Arms at the terminus. The latter closed, was gutted by fire and demolished. Route 10 to Compton Road had one pub only, the Compton Arms at the terminus, and en route there were two off licence shops. The short branch to the Gipton Estate had no pubs or cinemas, but both the Compton Road and Gipton trams did pass some in York Street. The Gipton cars also in York Road. Both these are covered in the York Road section. The Compton Arms no longer exists.

All the pubs in this section were fully licensed except for the Cricketers Arms, Sir Robert Peel and Kings Arms which sold beer only.

The Dewsbury Road tram route closed on 28 September 1957, Compton Road on 3 April 1954, Gipton on 23 April 1955 and that to Middleton on 28 March 1959.

**OLD RED LION, 2 and 4 Meadow Lane. Early 19th century - date.**
This pub is stated to be one of the oldest in Leeds dating from the late Georgian period and the style of architecture suggests this. The earliest reference found by the writer is in a directory of 1839. The building is grade 2 listed and still in business. Prior to about 1945 the pub was owned by McQuat's of Leeds.          Date: 25 September 1953.

**OLD GEORGE, 58 Meadow Lane. By 1798 – 1969.**
The Old George was a typical Georgian building and was mentioned in a Directory of 1798. It was demolished in the massive upheaval when the M1 Motorway was extended to Meadow Lane.                    Date: 3 September 1951.

**UNION TAVERN, 143 Meadow Lane. By 1839 - 1967.**
The Union Tavern, on the corner of Meadow Lane with Dewsbury Road, is to the right of the tram and is referred to in a Directory of 1839. It was a Georgian building and was unusual as it does not appear to have any identification on the front of the building. However, later in 1957 a large sign reading Union Tavern was added to the frontage. in 1899 it was owned by Samuel Allsopp and Sons, but was later a Samuel Smith's pub. It closed in 1967 and disappeared in 1968-9 along with other buildings in the area.                    Date: 5 January 1957.

**WHITE HOUSE HOTEL, 2-4 Dewsbury Road. By 1845-1969.**
The White House Hotel was a quite impressive building and carried a sculpted date of 1899. Its appearance was ruined by a crude brick-built gentlemen's urinal on an island in front of the building. It was a Ramsden's house and was a replacement for an earlier beer house in existence by 1845. It closed in 1969 and was demolished in 1971.

**PALACE CINEMA, 10 Meadow Road. 1915-1961.**
Also on the photograph is the Palace Cinema in Meadow Road, originally called the People's Picture Palace. It opened on 22 January 1915 and closed on 3 June 1961. Date: 12 November 1955.

**WHITE HOUSE HOTEL.**
Another view of the White House Hotel looking down Meadow Road towards Leeds. Date: 9 February 1957.

**JUNCTION HOTEL, 137 Dewsbury Road.  C 1817 – 2010.**
The Junction Hotel was an old inn situated at Hunslet Moor Bar at the start of the Leeds and Dewsbury Turnpike Road. The road was opened on 3 November 1817 and the pub was opened about that time or soon afterwards. It is listed in a Directory of 1826.  It latterly had a pub sign featuring a tram, and  closed in 2010 . It is currently used for flats.                                                                                                         Date: 27 September 1957.

**GREEN MAN INN, 190 Dewsbury Road. By 1834 - 1970.**
The Green Man was an old pub in existence by 1834 and situated on the corner of Vicar Street and Dewsbury Road. It was latterly a Ramsden's house.  It closed in 1970.                                                                            Date: 9 August 1956.

**NEW INN, 259 Dewsbury Road. 1842 – 2012.**
The New Inn was an old established building first licensed to Kelita Thompson on 29 August 1842. It was replaced by a new building in 1906-8 in ornate white faience. It closed in 2010, but reopened again in April 2012, closing again after about three months. It is a listed building and has been converted into an Asian supermarket.

Date: 19 September 1956.

**CRESCENT CINEMA, Dewsbury Road. 1921 – 1968.**
The New Crescent Super Cinema opened on 1 August 1921 and closed on 13 July 1968. The premises were then used for bingo and later Winston's Health and Leisure Centre, closed down in 2013. After 1953 the Crescent was used as a tram terminus.

Date: 13 October 1956.

**BROADWAY HOTEL, Dewsbury Road. Late 1939 - date.**
The Broadway is a large pub opened in late 1939 and is a John Smith's pub. It is still in business.

Date: 19 September 1957.

**TOMMY WASS HOTEL, 450 Dewsbury Road. Late 1920's to date.**
Thomas Wass was born in 1832 and built a farm house on the corner of Old Lane and Dewsbury Road. It later became refreshment rooms. Following the death of Asa Wass in 1924, the Melbourne Brewery bought the building and opened it as a pub in the late 1920's. By agreement with the Wass family the name was continued and the pub is still in business. Date: 28 September 1957, the last day of the Dewsbury Road tram service.

**MOOR HOUSE INN, 66 Moor Crescent. By 1854 – date.**
The Moor House Inn, the white building on the right, visible from Moor Road, was a beer seller's premises in 1854 the landlord being William Dutholt. In March 1879 it was taken over by Samuel Smith's Brewery of Tadcaster and is still in business.                                     Date: 25 March 1959.

**MIDDLETON ARMS, Middleton Park Circus. 1925 - 2011.**
The Middleton Arms was opened as a hotel in early July 1925. It together with the Mexborough Arms and Chained Bull marked a significant change in suburban pub design in Leeds. They were followed by similar buildings. The Middleton Arms had an impressive ball room. On 3 December 2011 it was seriously damaged in a fire and demolished in April 2012. At present there is an Aldi Supermarket (opened in the spring of 2014) on the site.
                              Date: 28 March 1959, the last day of the Middleton tram service.

**COMPTON ARMS, Compton Road. 1928 - 2002.**
There was only one pub on the Compton Road tramway route, the Compton Arms. It was a large impressive building built in 1928 and dominated Compton Road. Its clientele was mainly the workers at the nearby Montague Burton Clothing Factory. Following drugs abuse and other problems, it closed in 2002. After suffering vandalism and arson attacks it was demolished in March 2006.

There were two off licence shops on the Compton Road tramway route, both in Nippet Lane. The tram is passing a Dutton's off licence and in the distance is a Tetley's shop.                                    Date: 17 January 1954.

# TRAM ROUTE 14. CORN EXCHANGE TO ARMLEY, BRAMLEY AND STANNINGLEY.

For the purposes of this book, this section covers the tram route from the White Horse, at the junction of Wellington Road and Armley Road, to Stanningley.

Wellington Street and Wellington Road were traversed by the No.14 trams, but were also used by the No.4 trams to Kirkstall Abbey (Wellington Street only) and the Tong Road routes, Nos.15 and 16. Pubs on these roads are covered in the Tong Road section.

Proceeding from the White Horse Junction, there were two pubs on the lower end of Armley Road: The Albert Inn and the Albion. On the other side of the railway line were the Oak, visible from the tram and on the corner of Croton Place and Canal Street; Castleton, Scarborough Hotel, Rose and Crown, Old Golden Lion and the Nelson Hotel at the end of Armley Road.

The densely built up area of Armley ended at the bottom of Stanningley Road and there were only two pubs from there to Half Mile Lane: the Daisy Inn and the Brown Cow. In Stanningley Town Street there were the Waggon and Horses, Jug and Barrel, Old Roundabout Inn and the Fleece Hotel at the tram terminus.

There were two cinemas, the Clifton at Bramley Town End and the Pavilion at Half Mile Lane.

We have been unable to find photographs of trams passing the Oak (built by 1862, licensed 30 August 1867, closed C 1976)) or Castleton (closed about 1978), both of which were set back from the tramway, or the Jug and Barrel. The latter was not referred to in the directories by name, but as a beer seller's premises only.

The Daisy Inn, Waggon and Horses and Jug and Barrel are still in business.

The short section of tramway from the Pavilion Cinema at Half Mile Lane to Stanningley was abandoned on 3 January 1953. The remainder of the No. 14 tram route ceased operation on 3 October 1953.

**WHITE HORSE HOTEL, junction of Wellington Road and Armley Road. By 1817 – 1972.**
The White Horse Hotel was an old pub at an important junction and was in existence by 1817. It was acquired by Tetley's in September 1931 and was purchased by Leeds Corporation under a compulsory purchase order dated 30 November 1970 in connection with Phase 3 of the Inner Ring Road. This same order included five other pubs: The Wellington in Wellington Street, the Junction Hotel at the corner of Wellington Street and Kirkstall Road, the North Eastern in Wellington Street, the Leeds Arms in Westgate, and the Fisherman's Hut in West Street. In 1971-2 all the pubs listed were closed and demolished along with other property in the area.          Date: 16 August 1953.

**ALBERT INN, 76 Armley Road.  By 1888 – 1960's .**
This is the best photograph we have found of a tram passing the Albert Inn at the bottom of Armley Road.  It shows the pub sign only. The building was rather dilapidated and sold Hammond's Tower Ales. We have been unable to find any reference to the pub by name in the directories, telephone directories, Brewster Sessions or on the O.S. maps.  It  was a beer house, in existence by 1888 and closed in the 1960's.          Date: 16 August 1953.

**ALBION INN, 86 Armley Road. 1860's - 2009.**
The Albion dates from 1859 when Thomas Robinson bought land from the estates of Armley Hall. Between 1861 and 1866 he bought 26 houses and four shops. One of the shops was a beer house, which became the Fleece Inn in 1873 and adjacent was the Albion, a pub, about 1886. In 1898 both were bought by Peter Walker & Sons, brewers of Warrington. In 1919 they were merged into one pub, the Albion, and Walker's sold it to Tetley's in September 1925. It was damaged by a fire and closed in 2009 and was the last pub to remain open in Armley Road.  The building still exists and is currently used as workshop units.          Date: 16 August 1953.

**SCARBRO' HOTEL, 148 Armley Road. By 1880's - 1977.**
Armley Road with a John Smith's off licence on the corner of Parliament Place. The tram is passing the Scarbro'
Hotel, a Ramsden's house. The Scarbro' is another pub that is not referred to in the local directories by name. It is a
beer house only. The pub closed in July 1977. From 1974 to 1977 extensive demolition took place in Armley Road
from the Railway bridge to Branch Road, for the construction of the Armley Gyratory and a new approach road to
Armley. The Oak Inn, Castleton Hotel and Scarbro' Hotel disappeared. Date: 15 August 1953.

**ROSE AND CROWN, 196 Armley Road. By 1839 – 2009.**
The Rose and Crown was an old pub in existence by 1839. It was taken over by the Melbourne Brewery in May 1925
and closed in October 2008. It reopened in December, but closed again for good after three months. In April 2009 it
opened as an electrical shop. Date: 30 September 1953.

**GOLDEN LION, 204A Armley Road and 2 Canal Road. By 1874 – 2007.**
The Golden Lion on the left was in existence as a beer house in 1874 and closed in early 2007. It was demolished during October and November 2018.                                                    Date: 8 August 1953.

**NELSON HOTEL, 212 Armley Road. By 1823 - 2008.**
The earliest reference we have found to this pub is in 1823 when it was used for an auction sale. On 22 May 1894 it was purchased by a William Ledgard who leased it to his son Samuel in 1897. Samuel remained landlord of the pub until his death in 1952 and he was to become a legendary figure and notable as one of the major private bus operators in Leeds. The Nelson closed about October 2008 and on 1 November 2010 was opened as an Indian restaurant. The photograph shows the Nelson with three Ledgard buses parked outside.          Date: July 1964.

**CLIFTON CINEMA, 377 Stanningley Road. 1939 - 1961.**
The Clifton was situated at Bramley Town End and was a typical art deco style cinema of the 1930's. The Architect was William Illingworth & Son of Bradford. It was opened on 30 January 1939 and closed on 17 June 1961. It was used as a Howarth DIY centre and from 1977 used by Forest Products and later demolished. In the background of the photograph is Bramley tram depot opened in 1906. It was later a bus garage and closed in April 1969. By the end of June 1969 it had been demolished.                                                          Date: 19 September 1953.

**DAISY INN, 168 Stanningley Road. C 1836 – date.**
The Daisy Inn was built as a resting place on the new Wortley, Armley and Bramley Turnpike Road, or Armley Road and Stanningley Road, which opened in 1836. It was listed in directories by 1839 and was probably built either immediately before or after the turnpike opened. It is still in business.                                    Date: 3 July 1953.

**BROWN COW INN , 613 Stanningley Road. C 1836 – C 2007.**
The same remarks apply to this pub as for the Daisy above. Like the Daisy, it was typical of the vernacular style which had prevailed over the last 200 years or so. Unusually when the turnpike road was built dry stone walling was placed on each side and in the foreground can be seen an example which survived into the 1950's. The pub closed about 2007 and was later demolished.                                                      Date: 26 September 1953.

**PAVILION CINEMA, Stanningley Road. 1920 - 1970.**
The Pavilion Cinema was in a dominant location at the top of Stanningley Road. Designed by J.P. Crawford of Leeds, it had a facade of brick and white faience, popular in the 1920's. It opened on 28 February 1920 and closed on 5 April 1970. The building still exists and was at first used for bingo. About 2005 it was converted into offices.   Date: 1950.

**WAGGON AND HORSES, Town Street, Stanningley.      By 1839 - date.**
The Waggon and Horses was at the termination of the Wortley, Armley and Stanningley Turnpike Road and almost certainly dates from the opening of the turnpike road in 1836. As with the Daisy and Brown Cow, it appears in the directories for the first time in 1839. It was fully licensed from 26 August 1844 and is still in business.

Date: 23 August 1953.

**FLEECE HOTEL, Town Street, Stanningley.  By 1817 – C 2000.**
Bob Mack unintentionally took this fine photograph of the Fleece Hotel at Stanningley tram terminus in 1949. There was a beer house on the site by 1817 and this is most probably the original building. It obtained its first licence on 28 August 1863. It closed about 2000 or shortly before.

Date :15 April 1949.

A 1910 postcard showing a dual gauge Bradford tram designed for 4ft.0in. gauge on 4ft.8½ in. gauge Leeds rails.  It is passing the Old Roundabout Inn at 38 Town Street, Stanningley.  The Old Roundabout was very old, originally the Roundabout House, and was advertised to be let or sold in the Leeds Intelligencer of 9 December 1760. In the 1840's the landlord was Joseph Vickers who gave his name to Vickers Yard  and Vickers Place. The pub closed about 2012.

The same location on 6 July 2017.  The squat Wright Street Deck bus contrasts with the Edwardian "elegance" of the Bradford tram.   The vernacular stone houses, typical of Stanningley, have given way to low grade industrial buildings and anti-vandal fencing. A cycle track with cars parked on it takes up much of the width of the road.  By coincidence a 21st century youth walked into the picture contrasting with the smartly dressed man with umbrella. Sadly the derelict pub, almost certainly the building that existed in 1760, was demolished in April 2018 (postponed from November 2017) and nothing now remains of the 1910 scene. The pub site is currently a scrap metal salvage yard.

Interestingly the journey time from Bradford to Leeds by tram with about twice as many stops as the bus was 65 minutes. By bus in 2017, following almost the same route, it was 54 minutes, but due to congestion often exceeded the 1910 time.  Did things improve in 107 years?

# THE TONG ROAD TRAM ROUTES.

## TRAM ROUTES 15 CORN EXCHANGE TO WHINGATE AND 16 CORN EXCHANGE TO NEW INN.

The whole of the tram route from Wellington Bridge to New Inn and part of Whingate was heavily built up with working class and artisan housing. The "large modern suburb" of New Wortley was largely finished by 1853, but the housing in Tong Road was built about ten to fifteen years later.

In Wellington Street there were only two pubs on the tram route: the West Riding Hotel at City Square (included in the city centre section) and the North Eastern near Wellington Bridge. There was also the Great Northern Hotel, a residential hotel and outside the remit of this book.

In Wellington Road from the White Horse Junction to the Crown Hotel, New Wortley, there were five pubs all beer houses with the exception of the Queen. In order they were the Prince of Wales, Queen, Royal George, Albion Hotel, Spotted Cow and in addition the Main Line Club at the end of Copley Street. The Main Line Club sold John Smith's ales and was probably licensed to sell other drinks.

On Tong Road from the Crown Hotel to Whingate Junction there were four more pubs: the Beech Hotel – a beer house very close to the fully licensed Crown Hotel, the Cemetery Hotel, City Hotel, and Star Inn. On the branch to New Inn there was the New Inn at the tram terminus and in Whingate was the Commercial Hotel. We have not included the White Lion Hotel (closed 2009) which was opposite the Star Inn, but tucked away in a yard and not visible to the photographer.

There were two cinemas on Tong Road: the Crown Cinema at New Wortley and the Lyric Cinema further up Tong Road.

Still in business are the West Riding Hotel, Beech Hotel, Star Inn and Commercial Hotel.

We have been unable to find suitable photographs of the Prince of Wales, Queen, (first licensed 30 August 1854), City Hotel (closed December 1972), and the two cinemas.

The Tong Road tram routes ceased operation on 21 July 1956.

## NORTH EASTERN, 128 Wellington Street. By 1870 – 1971-2.
This pub was in existence by 1870, but we have found very little information. In 1971-2 it closed and was demolished to make way for stage 3 of the Inner Ring Road extension. In the tramway period it was licensed to sell beer only.                                              Date: 2 October 1954.

**ROYAL GEORGE, 84 Wellington Road.   By 1861 - C 1965.**
New Wortley became built up in the late 1840's and early 1850's and the Royal George, Queen and Prince of Wales originated at this time. In 1861 the Royal George was referred to as a beer house and remained as such throughout its life.  It was latterly an Ind Coope house and closed about 1965 in a slum clearance programme.  On the photograph the Royal George is on the left and the John Smith's pub in the background is the Prince of Wales at 72 Wellington Road.  Hidden by the tram at Nos. 74-78 Wellington Road was the Queen pub.  The Prince of Wales was bought by Leeds Corporation under a compulsory purchase order.                    Date: 11 September 1954.

**ALBION HOTEL, 90 Wellington Road.  By 1826 – C 1965.**
The Albion was an old pub and is listed in a 1826 directory. It appears to have been the first pub in Wellington Road and was probably built to serve the new Wellington and Tong Lane End Turnpike Road, completed between 1827 and 1829 and which began at New Wortley.  In 1965 the north side of Wellington Road was cleared in a comprehensive development which included new housing and multi-storey flats.            Date: 11 September 1954.

**SPOTTED COW,  81 later 106 Wellington Road.  By 1844 – C 1965.**
In existence by 1844, the Spotted Cow, between Clyde Street and Grange Street,  became a Tetley's pub in June 1939. The landlord in 1844 was Abraham Bateson. It closed in 1965 and was demolished as part of the Wellington Road slum clearance scheme.                                                       Date: 11 September 1954.

**MAIN LINE CLUB,  126 Wellington Road.  C 1950 – C 1965.**
In the 1930's this building on the corner of Copley Street, called Railway House, had been an auctioneer's premises, but after the 1939-45 war was used as an office by Main Line Football Pools. By 1954 it had become a railway social club selling John Smith's Ales. The building was demolished about 1965 in the Wellington Road comprehensive development scheme. The Main Line Club was relocated in premises in Pudsey Road and still exists.
                                                                         Date 11 September 1954.

**CROWN HOTEL, 2 Tong Road.     By 1839 – 2009.**
Although in a prominent position at the start of the new turnpike road to Tong Lane End, the earliest reference we
have found to the Crown is in a directory for 1839.  It closed in mid-2009. It was two doors away from the Beech
Hotel.  (see below).   The building still exists and is used for shops.                              Date: 1956.

**BEECH HOTEL, 8 Tong Road.  By 1870 – date.**
In the 1860's there was a beer retailer's premises on this site and by 1870 it was called the Beech Hotel.  In 1932 the
Melbourne Brewery opened a new building designed by Garside and Pennington.  It was typical of the style of
architecture fashionable for pubs and cinemas at this time. It has marble effect "Marmo" cladding and has an
unaltered "art deco" interior. It is Grade 2 listed and still in business. To the left of the tram is the Crown Cinema
(1919-1968) and to the right the Crown Hotel, also a Melbourne pub.                     Date: 11 September 1954.

**CEMETERY HOTEL, 67 Tong Road. 1864 – 1970.**
The Cemetery Hotel was opposite Grasmere Street, Tong Road. It opened as a beer house in 1864 the first landlord being Charles Stead. It was acquired by the Melbourne Brewery in December 1927 and closed in 1970, was demolished and replaced by a new pub on the same site called the White Rose. Date: 21 July 1956.

**STAR INN, 205 Tong Road. By 1817 – date.**
The Star Inn is an old pub and is listed in a directory of 1817. It had its own brewhouse and was taken over by Tetley's in June 1925. It is still in business. Date: 11 September 1954.

**THE NEW INN, 336 Tong Road. 1841 - 2009.**
Although the New Inn was a very ordinary "standard design" working class pub, in the tramway era it was probably one of the best known in Leeds. It was a tram terminus and trams showed "New Inn, Wortley" or "New Inn" on their destination indicators. On 31 August 1841 a licence was issued to John Carlton for the New Inn, Wortley Moor Side. It was taken over by the Melbourne Brewery in March 1928. It closed in May 2009 and was converted into flats.
Date: 18 April 1954.

**COMMERCIAL HOTEL, 142 Whingate. By 1864 – date.**
On the corner of Whingate and Wortley Road, the Commercial Hotel was in existence by 1864 the first landlord being William Atkinson. John Smith's Brewery of Tadcaster took over in March 1930. The Commercial Hotel is still trading.
Date: 11 September 1954.

# THE YORK ROAD TRAM ROUTES.

## TRAM ROUTES 18 CROSS GATES, 20 HALTON AND 22 TEMPLE NEWSAM.

Originally these tram routes were densely built up as far as Lupton Avenue on York Road, but by the 1950's most of the buildings on the inner part of the tram route had been demolished as part of a slum clearance programme. Some pubs, however, remained.

For the purposes of this book, in addition to York Road, we are covering the section of tramway from Kirkgate, New York Street, Harper Street, York Street and Marsh Lane to the Woodpecker Inn. There were three pubs on this section, the Brougham Arms on the corner of Kirkgate and Harper Street, the Old Royal Oak between KIrkgate and New York Street and the Lloyds Arms at the corner of York Street and Duke Street.

The Woodpecker was at the bottom of York Road, at the junction of York Road with Marsh Lane, New York Road and Burmantofts Street. On the lower part of York Road were three isolated pubs: the Fleece Inn, Hope Inn and Victoria Hotel. Near to the Hope Inn was Hemingway's Brewery. Then followed the White Horse Hotel, Shaftesbury Hotel, Dog and Gun and Melbourne in York Road and the Wykebeck Arms and Irwin Arms on the Halton and Temple Newsam section. The New Eagle was in Lupton Avenue adjacent to Torre Road tram depot and bus garage. The Fleece Inn and Victoria Hotel were licensed to sell beer only.

There were three cinemas: the Star and Shaftesbury on York Road and the Regal at Cross Gates tram terminus. Still existing are the Brougham Arms, renamed the Duck and Drake, White Horse (currently closed) and Wykebeck Arms.

We have been unable to find a suitable photograph of the Star Cinema which was set back and sideways to York Road.

The York Road tram routes, the last to operate in Leeds, were withdrawn on 7 November 1959.

**BROUGHAM ARMS, (later DUCK AND DRAKE), 43 Kirkgate. By 1839 – date.**
This Hammond's pub was in existence by 1839. It was renamed the Duck and Drake in the 1980's and is still in business.                                                      Date:  10 October 1959.

**OLD ROYAL OAK, 34 Kirkgate. By 1797 – 2010.**
This pub, at first called the Royal Oak then the Old Royal Oak, was very old and in existence by 1797. It was between Kirkgate and New York Street, the main small frontage being on Kirkgate, but there was also access from New York Street. It was taken over by John Smith's Brewery in December 1925 and this view shows the Magnet Ales, New York Street entrance on the left. The Masons Arms can be seen in the background (see page 9).　　Date 4 January 1954.

**LLOYDS ARMS, 50 York Street. By 1807 – 1995.**
The Lloyds Arms was an old pub mentioned in a Directory of 1807. The replacement building on the right of the photograph was of a rather unusual design built in 1891-2, the Architect being Walter Samuel Braithwaite of Leeds. It was treated with hostility by the Licensing Magistrates on the grounds that there were too many pubs in the area. The pub was taken over by John Smith's of Tadcaster and demolished in February and March 1995 for road improvements.　　Date: 1 June 1956.

**Woodpecker Inn, 1 York Road. By 1817 – 1990.**
The Woodpecker Inn was in an important and prominent position at the bottom of York Road and was a landmark in Leeds for over 170 years. The earliest reference we have found is in a Directory of 1817. The first building was on the north side of York Road and survived until 1938 when it was purchased by Leeds City Council for road widening. A replacement building was built on the southern side of the road and opened in October 1939. On 15 March 1941, in an extensive bombing raid on Leeds, the Woodpecker was destroyed, but later rebuilt. It lasted until 1990 when it was demolished this time for good to make way for a flyover at the junction. At the time of writing this location is still called the Woodpecker Junction.                                      Date: 30 July 1952.

**FLEECE INN, 30 York Road. 1913-1955.**
This is the best photograph we have been able to find of a tram passing the Fleece Inn at the bottom of York Road. The beer house was a little gem, an impressive Edwardian building built by the Albion Brewery, Leeds, and opened in January 1913. It was situated between Vincent Street and Plaid Row, had tiles to the lower part and brick, terra cotta and faience to the upper part of the building. On the front gable there was a large faience sculpted panel reading "Fleece Inn" and on the side a larger similar panel advertising the "Albion Brewery (Leeds) Ltd.". This is visible on the photograph but partly concealed by the Fleece Hotel sign. Unfortunately the building was the cause of a "tram pinch" and congestion in this part of York Road. The photograph was taken on 19 April 1954 and the building was demolished the following year.       In the background is the Hope Inn and on the left a derelict school.
                                                                                                Date: 19 April 1954.

**HOPE INN, 74 York Road.  C 1834 – 1969.**

The Hope Inn, on the corner of Upper Accommodation Road at its junction with York Road, was an old building dating from about 1834.  It was taken over by the Melbourne Brewery in January 1918.  On 28 October 1969 a Government grant was given for widening York Road between the Woodpecker Inn and Lupton Avenue.  The Hope and Victoria (see below) were closed and demolition and clearance took place from November 1969 to January 1970.  The widening began in April 1970 and following the road improvements the pub was replaced nearby with a new Hope Inn which still exists.                                                                          Date: 8 August 1959.

**J.W. HEMINGWAY'S BREWERY, All Saints Road, York Road.   By 1870 – 1967.**

Although the cyclists and pedestrians take centre stage, this is the only photograph we have been able to find which shows a tram and the complete unobstructed frontage of Hemingway's Brewery in York Road.  It is the large building to the right of Horsfield car 156 and was on the east side of Pontefract Lane not far from the Hope Inn.

By 1870 John William Hemingway had a small malt house nearby at 4 All Saints Road.  The style of architecture suggests that the building illustrated was built before the First World War certainly no later than about 1920. Hemingway's was acquired by Tetley's in 1967 and the York Road building became redundant. The old brewery was bulldozed away in 1969-1970 with the Hope Inn, Victoria Hotel and other buildings to make way for the widening of York Road.                                                                          Date: 8 August 1959.

**VICTORIA HOTEL, 79 York Road. By 1857 – 1969.**
Situated on the east side of Freehold Street at its junction with York Road, this pub was in existence by 1857. The first landlord was Andrew Jennings, and latterly it was a Dutton's house. The white faience extension to the ground floor appears to have been added in the late 1920's or early 30's. The pub was demolished to make way for the widening of York Road.                                                     Date: 20 June 1959.

**VICTORIA HOTEL, 79 York Road.**
Looking down York Road towards the Leeds City centre with the Victoria Hotel on the right. Because of the demolition of the adjacent buildings, in the 1950's the east side of the building was a large white painted wall.
                                                                                    Date 26 February 1955.

**NEW EAGLE, Lupton Avenue.  1937 – 1998.**
The New Eagle was on the corner of Lupton Avenue and Torre Road. The Torre Road tram depot and bus garage were opened in 1937 and the New Eagle was opened in June of that year by John Smith's Brewery of Tadcaster.  It was designed in the art deco style and is a good example of this type of architecture.  It had a symmetrical frontage with a central pole topped by a large gilded golden eagle.  Torre Road Garage closed in 1996.  The New Eagle closed in 1998, was demolished and the site is currently used for car parking.  The works tram is a rail grinder and looking on is a tram conductress.                                                          Date 27 July 1958.

**WHITE HORSE HOTEL,  360 York Road.  By 1849 – date.**
The White Horse Hotel on the right is mentioned in a directory of 1849.  At the present time (2019) the building has been closed since about 2016, but is not  boarded up.                                                          Date C 1937.

**SHAFTESBURY CINEMA, York Road. 1928 – 1975.**
The Shaftesbury Cinema on the right at the Junction of Harehills Lane and York Road, opened on 20 October 1928 and closed on 28 June 1975. The Architect was J.P.Crawford of Leeds. Most of the building was demolished in 1980, but the entrance facade and the part facing Harehills Lane still remains. The photograph is taken looking towards Leeds. **Date: 1959.**

**SHAFTESBURY HOTEL. C 1926 – C 2006.**
Looking towards York on the left hand side is the corner of the Shaftesbury Cinema. The Shaftesbury Hotel is in the left background and was built about the middle 1920's, and lasted rather longer than the cinema. It was a Melbourne pub and we believe it was built by this firm. It closed in 2006-7 and was demolished in the latter part of 2008. It was included in the 2009-2010 telephone directory! It was replaced by a care home. **Date 27 March 1955.**

**SHAFTESBURY HOTEL.**
Another view of the Shaftesbury Hotel showing the front of the building in 1965. Tetley's bought out the Melbourne Brewery in 1960 and the pub is displaying a Tetley's sign.                    Date: 17 July 1965.

**DOG AND GUN, 579 later 601 York Road. By 1822 - 2014.**
The Dog and Gun was an old pub, the earliest reference we have found is dated 1822, but parts of the building are stated to date from the eighteenth century. In 1936 it was extended on the west side to cater for new housing in the area. It closed about September 2014 and reopened as a "Family Shopper" store on 15 March 2015. This enterprise was unsuccessful and lasted just over a year. At the time of writing, 2019, the building is being converted into housing units.                    Date: 26 September 1954.

**WYKEBECK ARMS, 59 Selby Road. 1939 – date.**
The Wykebeck Arms was built in 1938-1939 and, in order to obtain a licence, on 21 October 1939 the licences of the Royal Hotel, in South Accommodation Road and those of the Stag Hotel and Greyhound Inn in York Road were surrendered.   The pub is still in business.                                    Date: 26 September 1959.

**IRWIN ARMS, Halton.  By 1853 -  C 2002-3.**
The rear view of the Irwin Arms was visible from the tramway and not easy to photograph.  It was an old pub and in existence by 1853. In January 1926 it was acquired by John Smith's Brewery, Tadcaster.  In 1938-9 it was  replaced by the building on the photograph.  It closed about 2002-3 and was demolished in May 2006 and replaced with a supermarket.  It appeared in the telephone directory until 2009-2010!                    Date:  30 October 1959.

**MELBOURNE HOTEL, York Road. 1928 – 1988.**
The Melbourne on the corner of York Road and Foundry Lane was opened in 1928. It was a typical 1920's large suburban public house and closed 60 years later in 1988. It was demolished and replaced by a Burger King facility.
Date: 1959.

**REGAL CINEMA, Cross Gates. 1936 – 1964.**
Built in 27 weeks, the Regal had a massive car park accommodating 400 cars. The Architect was A.V. Montague of Leeds. It opened on 16 November 1936 and closed on 11 January 1964. The premises were demolished over the following month or so to make way for a G.E.M. supermarket opened on 13 May 1965.    Date: 25 January 1956.

# TRAM ROUTES 25, HUNSLET AND 26/27, BELLE ISLE.

In this section we are covering the section of tramway from Swinegate via Mill Hill, Neville Street and Great Wilson Street to Hunslet Lane and Hunslet Road, the branch to Hunslet and then Belle Isle.

On the tram route from Swinegate, there were the Prince of Wales, Black Lion (by 1798 – date) and Scarbrough Hotel at Mill Hill, followed by the Clarendon Hotel in Neville Street and the Victoria Inn just visible in Water Lane. In Great Wilson Street was the Falcon Inn before Hunslet Lane was reached. In Hunslet Lane there was the White Lion and in Hunslet Road the Black Bull Hotel, New Inn, Mulberry, Royal George, Prince Albert and the Swan Hotel at Swan Junction. In Low Road was the Wellington and in Thwaite Gate the Old Red Lion and Crooked Billet. There was one pub in Waterloo Road: the Garden Gate and then the Anchor Inn, Railway Hotel, Bay Horse Hotel and on Belle Isle Road, the Belle Isle Hotel and Grey Goose. On the return journey to Leeds the trams passed the Adelphi at Bridge End. Near to the Wellington Hotel in Low Road, was the Regal Cinema. We have also included in this section the Red House in Meadow Lane and the former McQuat's brewery also in Meadow Lane. They were to be seen from the tram returning from Middleton on the 26 circular route.

The Prince of Wales, (currently called the Moot Hall Arms), Black Lion (currently the Head of Steam), Scarbrough Hotel, Garden Gate, Bay Horse, (currently the New Bay Horse), and Adelphi still exist. In 1988 the Belle Isle Hotel was opened as the Victoria House Residential Home, and the Grey Goose is a shop.

We have been unable to find suitable photographs of the Prince Albert, (a former McQuat's pub see below, by 1842 - C 1970) Railway Hotel (set back from Balm Road), Bay Horse Hotel, (built by 1843 and also set back from Balm Road), Belle Isle Hotel and Grey Goose, (C 1958 to 25 September 2008). The Belle Isle Hotel was in Low Grange Crescent and difficult to see from the tram.

Tram routes 26 and 27 to Belle Isle were withdrawn on 28 March 1959 and route 25 to Hunslet on 18 April the same year.

**PRINCE OF WALES, 11 Mill Hill. By 1870 - date.**
By 1853 there was a beer house on this site and in 1870 it was referred to as the Prince of Wales. John Smith's Brewery of Tadcaster took over the premises in August 1881 and the building on the photograph appears to date from this period. It is assumed that it was built by John Smith's. The pub was threatened with closure in 2008 because of a dispute regarding the tied lease. This restricted the landlord to selling a limited number of drinks and has always been a pub problem. The pub could only sell drinks supplied by the brewery owning the building. Many pubs now are free houses and can sell any drinks that they wish. The Prince of Wales is currently called the Moot Hall Arms and is still in business.                     Date: 18 April 1959, the last day of the Hunslet tram route.

**SCARBROUGH HOTEL, Bishopgate Street. 1823 – date.**
The Scarbrough Hotel was built about 1823 and is named after Henry Scarbrough, the first landlord (1823 – 1847). It is known locally as the Scarbrough Taps and is still in business.    Workmen are clearing snow from the pavement.
Date 21 December 1955.

**CLARENDON HOTEL, 30 Victoria Road. 1840 – C 1973.**
The Clarendon Hotel was a new building licensed to Thomas Parker on 1 September 1840 and was latterly a John Smith's pub.  It closed about 1973 and was demolished about 2002 to make way for the Bridgwater Place tower block, on which construction began in 2004.    Just visible to the right of the Clarendon, the white painted building is the Victoria Inn in Water Lane.
Date: 12 July 1955.

**VICTORIA INN, 56-58 Water Lane . By 1866 – C 1953.**
The former Victoria Inn is the white building to the right of the Clarendon Hotel above . It was in existence as a beer house by 1866 and taken over by John Smith's Brewery, Tadcaster, in March 1938.   It closed about 1953 and the following year the premises were occupied by B.C.F. Transport Co.Ltd. whose name appears on the building in this photograph.                                                                                                                    Date 1955.

**FALCON INN, 7 Great Wilson Street. By 1849 – 1966.**
The Falcon was near the corner of Church Cross Street  with Great Wilson Street. It was listed in a directory of 1849 and in March 1921 was taken over by Tetley's Brewery.   It closed in 1966.                              Date: 2 March 1956.

**WHITE LION, Hunslet Lane.  By 1837 – 1969-70.**
The White Lion was on the corner of Hunslet Road with Hunslet Lane and was in existence by 1837.   In September 1922 it was acquired by Tetley's.   It closed about 1969-70.                                              Date: 24 January 1959.

**WHITE LION.**
The White Lion looking towards Hunslet.  It is concealing the Black Bull Hotel (see below), and Wallace Arnold's coach yard,  which are to the left of the Feltham tram in the distance.                      Date 24 January 1959.

**BLACK BULL HOTEL, 91 Hunslet Road. By 1842 - 1971-2.**
On the corner of Black Bull Street and Hunslet Road, the Black Bull Hotel was in existence by 1842 and was taken over by John Smith's Brewery, Tadcaster, in September 1896. It closed about 1971-2.          Date: 24 January 1959.

**NEW INN, 127-129 Hunslet Road. By 1842– 1970.**
A beer house by 1842 the New Inn was on the corner of Sayner Road and was latterly a Ramsden's pub. After many applications, on 29 August 1866 Elbourn Barker succeeded in obtaining a licence. It closed in 1970.
Date: 13 March 1959.

**MULBERRY HOTEL,   186 later 152 Hunslet Road. By 1855 - 2012.**
The Mulberry Hotel also called the Mulberry Tree, was licensed by 1855 and  acquired by the Melbourne Brewery in May 1890.  It closed in 2012.                                                      Date: 16 March 1959.

**ROYAL GEORGE HOTEL,  32 later 201 Hunslet Road. By 1839 – 1969.**
Near the corner of Hunslet Road with South Accommodation Road, the earliest date we have found for the Royal George Hotel is 1839.  It was a fine Georgian building and acquired by John Smith's Brewery in October 1896. It was sold to Leeds Corporation in 1968, closed the following year and demolished for road improvements.     Date:  1959.

**SWAN HOTEL, 1 Waterloo Road. By 1834 – 1971.**
This pub was originally called the Swan with Two Necks and was in a prominent location at the junction of Hunslet Road, Low Road and Waterloo Road. The pub is listed in a directory of 1834 and became a Melbourne pub in March ~~1878. About 1900~~ it was impressively rebuilt by the Melbourne Brewery and latterly sold Ramsden's Ales. The Swan closed in 1971.
Date: 5. July 1958.

**SWAN HOTEL.**
A closer view of the Swan Hotel on the right showing the Victorian detailing of the facade.      Date: 13 March 1959.

**REGAL CINEMA, 50 Low Road, 1913 - 1959.**
This cinema was opened as the Pavilion on 3 January 1913. The Architects were Chadwick & Watson of Leeds. On 6 January 1930 it changed its name to the Regal and closed on 30 May 1959. It became a motor car showroom. The photograph shows a group of children leaving the cinema and waiting to cross the road. The former cinema was later demolished.
                                                                                    Date: 23 August 1958.

**WELLINGTON, Low Road. 18ᵗʰ century -2009.**
The Wellington was next door to the Regal Cinema, but the tram is concealing most of the cinema. As early as 1760 there was a pub on the site called the Organ and in November 1825 it was sold and referred to as the Wellington. Tetley's took over in May 1892. The white faience building on the photograph dates from the late 1920's / early thirties. The Wellington closed in late 2009 and is currently "mydentist", an orthodontic centre.
                                                                                    Date: 23 August 1958.

**WELLINGTON, Low Road. 18th century -2009.**
A view of The Wellington looking towards Hunslet.                    Date 3 November 1956.

**OLD RED LION, 49 Thwaite Gate. By 1817 – C 2000.**
Near to the Hunslet tram terminus, the Old Red Lion was in existence by 1817. In December 1920 it was acquired by
the Melbourne Brewery.  It was demolished  about 2000.  The Crooked Billet (see below) can be seen in the distance.
Date: 3 November 1956.

**CROOKED BILLET, 61 Thwaite Gate. By 1813 – 2014.**
In the Leeds Intelligencer of 19 April 1813 the Crooked Billet was advertised to let and described as "old established". It closed in 2014 and by April 2016 had been demolished.     **Date: 31 August 1955.**

**GARDEN GATE, Waterloo Road. By 1833 – date.**
This Grade 2* listed building is a product of that very short period of highly decorative pub architecture that was fashionable around 1900 at the height of the art nouveau, and built of brick, terra cotta and glazed tiles, believed to be supplied by the Burmantofts Pottery. There was a pub on the site by 1833 and the present building was completed in 1902. In September 1901 a licence for the new building was granted. It was designed by Architect W. Mason Coggill of Stourton and was acquired by Ind Coope in 1922 and Tetley's in the 1960's. Waterloo Road was closed in October 1976, but the pub proudly stands.     **Date: 16 March 1959.**

**ANCHOR INN, 94 Church Street. By 1817 – 1977.**
The Anchor Inn was an old pub and is listed in a 1817 directory. In March 1926 it was taken over by Tetley's Brewery, closed on 27 March 1977 and was subsequently demolished.                    Date: March 1959.

**OLD RED HOUSE, Meadow Lane. By 1849 - C 1969.**
On their return to the city centre trams on the 26 circular route passed the Red House pub in Meadow Lane. It was built by 1849 and acquired by John Smith's Brewery of Tadcaster in May 1896. It was sold in 1968 under a compulsory purchase order to Leeds Corporation and disappeared the following year when motorway works were carried out.                    Date: 28 September 1957.

**McQUAT'S, 33 Meadow Lane. By 1872 – C 1945.**

This interesting building adjacent to the South Market in Meadow Lane was built about 1871 and opened by the following year as the New Cross Inn. Not long afterwards it was renamed the South Market Hotel. It closed about 1901-2 and appears to have been unoccupied for several years. By 1908 it had been acquired by wine and spirits merchants, the McQuat brothers who converted part of it into a small brewery brewing strong ale. McQuat's expanded and are stated to have owned nine pubs in Leeds. About 1945 McQuat's were bought out by Samuel Smith's Brewery of Tadcaster. McQuat's brewery closed, but the building was used for a time as Samuel Smith's Leeds Office, and was later a vulcanising works. McQuat's former building was demolished in the late 1960's. Note the Adelphi (see below) to the left of the tram.                                                   Date: 1957.

**ADELPHI, 30 Dock Street, Bridge End. 1838 – date.**

The Adelphi was an old inn granted its first licence on 3 September 1838. The licensee was Elizabeth Oates who owned the premises. It was replaced by the present building in 1901, the Architect being Thomas Winn of Leeds. It was acquired by the Melbourne Brewery in July 1925 and became a Tetley's pub in 1960.        Date: 21 March 1959.